I0647726

BAG
OF
HAMMERS

BAG OF HAMMERS

EDWARD RICHE

Breakwater Books
P.O. Box 2188, St. John's, NL, Canada, A1C 6E6
www.breakwaterbooks.com

Copyright © 2017 Edward Riche
ISBN 978-1-55081-686-0

All Rights Reserved. No part of this publication may be reproduced, stored in a retrieval system or transmitted, in any form or by any means, without the prior written consent of the publisher or a licence from The Canadian Copyright Licensing Agency (Access Copyright). For an Access Copyright licence, visit www.accesscopyright.ca or call toll free to 1-800-893-5777.

A CIP catalogue record for this book is available from Library and Archives Canada.

We acknowledge the support of the Canada Council for the Arts, which last year invested $153 million to bring the arts to Canadians throughout the country. We acknowledge the financial support of the Government of Canada and the Government of Newfoundland and Labrador through the Department of Tourism, Culture, Industry and Innovation for our publishing activities.

Breakwater Books is committed to choosing papers and materials for our books that help to protect our environment.

Also by Edward Riche

Novels
Rare Birds
The Nine Planets
Easy To Like
Today I Learned It Was You

Plays
Possible Maps
List of Lights
To Be Loved
Hail
The Pillow Trade
Dedication

For Frances

CONTENTS

IN NEWFOUNDLAND, IT'S MORE THAN A POLAR VORTEX

I gnore what you might have seen on those glorious Newfoundland and Labrador tourism ads or on *Republic of Doyle*, the weather here is the most foul in the Confederation. Canadians all over fancy they have an inhospitable climate. Dey knows nudding. Sure Winnipeg is colder, and remote mountain passes in British Columbia snowier and...well, nowhere is windier...but we can brag about being colder, snowier and windiest all at once. I wonder if we are not the only place on the planet that can have raging gales in a heavy fog. So it was last week, that after a long, very cold snap the temperature climbed to −15°C, the gusts stretched to

110 km/h, 40 centimetres of snow fell and the arse went out of her. Newfoundland blew a fuse. The lights went out.

Major winter blackouts get named here, like prize fights. There was "Blackout '94" when many were without power for as long as five days. The outage was shorter this time but we've grown softer, so this recent event has been unofficially dubbed "Blackout 2014" and, befitting the times, got hashtagged #DarkNL.

There is no one alive who knows prosperity in Newfoundland. Forever in decline we learned to do it well. Want made us more communal than most Canadians. We sublimated despair in song and stories. We enjoyed small things and the natural world, a play at the LSPU Hall and trouting.

Newfoundland and Labrador is booming now and nobody possesses the kit to fit. No one is prepared to manage prosperity. Officials admit that owing to years of near bankruptcy our infrastructure is obsolete and derelict and the stresses applied by a thrumming economy are testing its tolerance. When the extreme weather conditions came main cogs in the electrical system of the island (despite the abundance of energy stored in Labrador's high water we are unattached to the North American grid) failed. The articulate and sober head-in-chief of the power-generating utility, Ed Martin, explained that 88 per cent of the McMansions mushrooming around St. John's were built with electric heating and that the ancient network he runs was taxed to breaking by the usage surge in keeping them warm enough to make the inhabitants dopey.

Everywhere we are experiencing the symptoms of unmanaged expansion. Roads are crumbling under the load and choking with the unnecessary pick-up trucks that are the essential costume of an oil play. The flights are full and you can't get a table at an overpriced restaurant. Parking in the downtown of St. John's has become Parisian. Those in charge have responded by gleefully adding to the load, green-lighting ever more subdivisions and industrial parks. A vast development to the west of St. John's promoted by a former premier and so known as "Dannistan" was approved despite the grave concerns of planners. Without adequate transportation arteries in and out, the Dannistanis could be trapped in there without municipal water. What odds, a "have" province has gotta have it.

Kathy Dunderdale has proven a competent and honest premier but a dreadful communicator. She comes off as a vice principal hectoring a dim and fidgety grade four boy. Over the radio (blackouts become radio events) you can hear her wagging a finger at you. She told a dirty, agitated populace that there was no "crisis" when they were shivering in the dark watching their pipes burst. It was semantics; "crisis" for Premier Dunderdale is the Fall of Khartoum with giant spiders. For the electorate it was hours of cold gloom, elderly residents rescued from chronic-care facilities, carbon monoxide poisonings and school closures. She was nowhere to be seen in the first days of the "not a crisis."

A newly minted junior minister (and actual Boy Scout) Steve Kent flubbed his role as Alexander Haig, stepping in front of the microphones not to say he was in charge but that other levels of government were doing something. Ms. Dunderdale wasn't popular going into this mess and handled it poorly. It's consensus that her latest failure to hear the citizenry and respond will be one of her last.

This must be understood in the context of Newfoundland and Labrador being a self-proclaimed energy warehouse. The hydroelectric project at Muskrat Falls on the Lower Churchill comes with a sub-sea cable that will connect the island to the main and there are untold billions of BTUs still untapped under the Grand Banks. But as the last candle flickered and batteries in the radio ran down, all that reputed juice was cold comfort.

Originally published in *The Globe and Mail,* January 7, 2014.

THE
MUSKRAT FALLS
FESTIVAL OF THE
ARTS

The boondoggle that is The Muskrat Falls Festival of the Arts is now of such dimensions that the Government must immediately call an inquiry into the troubled microproject.

The three day celebration of Art and Culture was to cost $26,000 but overruns will see that nearly double to $40,000.

Delays in booking travel for the artists appearing at the festival mean that some will be arriving a full day ahead of the event and each incurring an extra day of Arts NL (formerly The Newfoundland and Labrador Arts Council) stipulated per diem of $49.00. Only because hotel rooms were not available on short notice were the artists billeted for that night with festival volunteers, otherwise the event would have borne the cost of the extra night's lodging, for as many as nine people, at Hotel North.

Firing the previous artistic director after she had resigned means the festival is responsible for both her taxi fare to the airport and a meal voucher for a Normie Special or Hot Wings at Jungle Jim's in Goose Bay.

Concerns remain that the stage, at an elevation of almost one metre, is not stable, and might collapse under a 5,000 year Running the Goat event. Despite several theatre technicians and three actors jumping up and down on the stage to test its reliability, the best we can get from the project managers is, "I dunno, suppose it's okay."

The visual art exhibition tied to the festival is signatory to extortionate VANL-CARFAC artist fees, resulting in some visual artists receiving as much as $372.00 for the two-week long exhibition of their work.

A Post-it note from a stage hand warning that costs for the festival were spiralling out of control was reportedly given to festival organizers but blew out a car window before being read.

The Minister of Tourism, Industry and Innovation's tweet that an audit is not being undertaken because no one could be arsed is unacceptable.

The decision to sanction the festival was likely an impulsive response to years of our talent being exported to Canada at exceedingly low rates, but that is no excuse for the commitment of thousands of taxpayers' dollars to keep our threatened culture on life support.

Arts and culture events such as the festival overwhelmingly feature and attract young people but we live in a province known to have a rapidly ageing population.

Defenders of the event say that arts funding is the lowest cost option to save Newfoundland and Labrador but these are the same people calling for a doubling of funding to Arts NL, a decision that will cost every citizen of the province AN EXTRA THIRTY-THREE CENTS PER MONTH!

While arts and culture give meaning to life in Newfoundland and Labrador, are a central plank of the Government's efforts to diversify the economy, add considerable value to the place as a destination for tourists, and attract and retain a younger demographic, it's going to take the province minutes if not hours to pay off this foolhardy venture.

Originally published as "Audit ArtsNL" in *The Overcast*, August 1, 2017.

PAUL WAS THE WALRUS

Sir Paul McCartney, a former bassist for The Beatles, has come, like a good Briton, to a former colony to pronounce on a barbaric practice of the natives—the hunting, for skins and meat, of seals. His appearance lends credence to the claim, by his onetime band mate John Lennon, that "the walrus was Paul." Mr. McCartney probably empathizes with his fellow flippereds.

I'm old enough to remember Brigit Bardot and Tanya Tucker coming round here to provide their expertise. But Paul McCartney is definitely the biggest fish, so to speak, to weigh in on the matter.

Those groups opposing the seal hunt off
Newfoundland and in the Gulf of St. Lawrence
are grateful for the McCartney endorsement and
mightily relieved. They can put the debacle that was
last year's protest behind them.

The most dogged of the anti-sealing operations
is The Sea Shepherd Society, an organization viewed
by most here in Canada's Happy Province as little
more than a fund-raising engine for its master, one
Paul Watson. You will recognize the zaftig Watson
by his shock of white hair and ample lips. He is
usually clad in Captain's casuals—epaulettes on
the shoulders of woollen knits—of his own design.
(The more mainstream friends-of-wildthings outfits
are uncomfortable allies of Mr. Watson, and would
never want his actions to be seen as representative of
their cause. Greenpeace, once the hunt's chief opponent, has left it pretty much alone now for years.)

Last sealing season The Sea Shepherd Society's
Ship, the aptly named *Farley Mowat*, turned out to
be a boat that wouldn't float. There was a hole in
her, a puncture in the hull very briefly and uncon-
vincingly posited as the handiwork of saboteurs.
Failure to bung this aperture spoiled the heretofore
perfect record for rescue and remediation of no less

a figure than MacGyver...or at least the fellow that played him on television. Richard Dean Anderson joked that he could not assist because he had not brought his writers with him. I've written for television and was impressed, at the very least, by this degree of self-awareness. The *Farley Mowat* tooled around Newfoundland waters for a brief interval getting beaten up by the ice, the team aboard hastily drew the same conclusions they had for years and, having failed to even witness the sorts of things they meant to forestall, headed south to Bermuda. Ahoy!

Having not *actually* witnessed last year's hunt did not stop Barbara Stewart, a freelancer working for The *Boston Globe*, from reporting about it in goriest detail. From the comfort of a motel room, dutifully informing her readership in New England of the mass slaughter underway, she failed to realize that the commencement of the event had been postponed on account of weather. The *New York Times* organization, owners of the Beantown organ, while accustomed to its reporters fabricating things, sacked Babs.

Happily none of the sealers got suckered into doing something alarming sanguinary for the cameras. Any of the spectacle you might have seen on television—the plentiful blood startling the white ice pans—was likely stock footage. The sealers have learned better how the game is played and will no longer mug, with raised gaff, for the visitors. We're barbarians down here, you know, but we're media savvy barbarians now. I was worried that a figure of McCartney's stature, with the mere promise of appearing at a dance or soup-supper in one of our remote out-harbours, even for just a single set with a local band, could coax a star-struck swiler to "beat the meatles" for the cause. Luckily he wanted nothing to do with us.

Most damaging to the protest last year was the revelation that among the crew of the *Farley Mowat* was Dr. Jerry Vlasak, a radical anti-vivisectionist Los Angelino who advocates the assassination of scientists involved in animal testing. Captain Watson danced around this for a few days, first standing by his man but finally, finding Vlasak too great a liability, cut the doctor loose, even removing him from the Sea Shepherd Society's board of directors. The Newfoundland variety of human life is particularly low in Vlasak's estimation. Complaining of one press report, Vlasak said that he "didn't expect much of a Newfie." We really hate that "Newfie" shit down here.

Imagine if Paul McCartney writes a protest song and uses the term "Newfie." That could really hurt.

Threats of violence from people who love animals to the sole exclusion of Homo sapiens aren't new. Some years ago a funny bit about the anti-sealing crowd ran on "The Great Eastern," a CBC Radio show in which I had a hand. It elicited numerous phone messages of righteous indignation, some promising the ice-picking and skull-smashing of the so-called comedy writers responsible. This season Paul Watson and his gang posted, on the Sea Shepherd Society website, the home phone number and mailing address of sealer Rendell Genge so that supporters might call and terrorize the man and his family. The provision of Mr. Genge's wife's name was an additional aide to those who wanted to personalize their voiced wish to see her skinned alive. Now Paul McCartney once sang "All You Need Is Love" and it was John who wanted to be counted-in for the destruction on "Revolution," so I'm sure he doesn't support that sort of thing.

Given the long propaganda campaign, city folk can be forgiven for mistaking the plight of the harp seal for that of the Bengal tiger, the Newfoundland Pine Marten or the Northern Cod. But the seals now outnumber Newfoundlanders about 10 to 1. If demographic trends don't soon change drastically, and the seals continue to thrive, their population will expand as Newfoundlanders vanish. We'll soon be for the stock footage too. Jerry Vlasak will be relieved.

A welcome counterpoint to the noise of the protesters last year was Anne Troake's NFB produced film, *My Ancestors Were Rogues and Murders*, an elegiac piece which used the life and death of her cousin Gary Troake, one of sealing's most articulate advocates, to meditate on the role sealing has played in the life of families, like the Troakes, of the north east coast. The film was the big hit at the St. John's Women's Film Festival. It predictably provoked the ire of Paul Watson who responded by describing Newfoundlanders as a "blight and a curse" who "... debased Canada when they joined the nation in 1949...." Ms Troake had a brick pitched through a window of her home one midnight.

I've been angered by some of Paul McCartney's work after he left The Beatles. "Silly Love Songs" made me want to throw a brick through the window of one his castles but I restrained myself.

My family, the Riches, have been involved in sealing for at least four or five generations. None, as far as I know, of the paternal progenitors were actually swilers—out nerving the ice floes. They were not tanners, nor middlemen of any sort, nor merchants. They were too hard-up to be even chandlers. No, my family has been and remains merely devoted eaters of seal, gastronomic pleasure-takers, phocid gourmets.

In my family's long love affair with seal cookery, my great-grandmother Riche, whom I never met, stands out as a particularly passionate figure. A formidable woman with a striking resemblance to Winston Churchill, she was the go-to midwife in the east end of "Sin Jahns" at the turn of the last century. A couple of my uncles, Paul and the late Eric, told how, when the first sealing vessels arrived to St. John's in the spring, her mouth would literally start to water and she would send one of her grandchildren off to purchase the first, most dear, flippers ashore. Paul told me, just the other day, that she would cut flesh from the seal the moment it came in the door, eating it raw, the blood running down her chin. I don't think this was bad table manners. She was, after a long Newfoundland winter, likely suffering from a vitamin or mineral deficiency that compelled her to such behaviour.

Some of her ancestors were Inuit so maybe she just liked it that way.

My wife is from Nova Scotia, some of her ancestors are Palatinate Germans, and she is not a fan. She can't "go" seal at all. My theory is that one cannot, late in life, make seals' distinctly fishy taste profile jibe with its excessive—the red of the flesh veers to black—meatiness. The common murr, the sea bird known here as turr, is another delicacy that challenges this expectation of taste. With a diet consisting primarily of capelin, their flesh takes on a piscine attribute. To the tongue turr seems neither fish nor fowl, but rather both at once. Ferran Adria would be ecstatic.

These days the smell and taste of seal is muted. When I was a boy they were purchased directly from the sealers who had worked on the large vessels. The harbour apron where the sealing ships tied up was transformed into a temporary, open-air butchery. This seal had "seasoned" in the time taken returning from the front, the blubber coming to possess a funky rancidity. You had to be particular when cleaning it to trim every last bit of this "high" fat from the exterior, a task aided by plunging the meat into a bath of water with bread-soda (sodium bicarbonate) making the trace strands more visible and subduing the perfume. These days the boats involved in the fishery have such whiz-bang modern refrigeration systems aboard that the raw meat at market has a delicate scent. While the smell of seal cooking is distinct, it certainly doesn't linger in the house like it used to.

What was once called "The Greatest Hunt in the World" is no longer prosecuted by large ships under merchant flags. The numbers harvested are a tiny fraction of what they once were. The white-coats, the dew-eyed "baby seals" that attracted so much sympathy from so far away, that drew the outraged likes of Bridget Bardot to our chilly shores, are no longer taken. These days the meat comes from the older Raggedy Jacks. I now buy my flippers at either of two local seafood shops or at Belbin's, a family grocery in the east end. They are sold on little Styrofoam trays and tightly wrapped in cellophane.

Even the freshest seal meat has a pronounced flavour. It is too strong to be matched with any sauce. There is virtually no wine to have "with." Manzanilla sherry can handle it, but they do nothing for one another. It is best accompanied by strong tea. If one must drink, then dark rum after.

At my Grandmother Riche's house, a meal of flippers was usually preceded by an appetizer of "hands," the terminal end of the seal's flipper, so named because of their resemblance to the human appendage. These, after having been boiled, were served cold. The cooked connective tissue of the hands was a greyish white and slightly gelatinous. The texture and pleasure in eating them resembles that taken from the duck feet on offer at your regular dim sum. I never see "hands" for sale anymore, or hearts, which were sold, floating in blood, out of old 10-gallon salt-beef buckets.

Mainlanders inexplicably find the sound of "flipper pie" funny. It's a meat pie like most others, simply slowly braised meat in a gravy covered by a pastry. While I feel I can cook flippers as well as my grandmother (this is the boldest statement I have ever written), I have never equalled her in the preparation of the "paste," the simple biscuit dough that covers the savoury. Hers was at once light and substantive, perhaps two inches thick, moist below its crusty carapace. She would place two or three over-turned tea cups in the roaster to keep the cooking pastry raised so it would not soak up all the delicious *jus*. Seal makes the very best gravy.

Flippers are first seared and then put in the pan with a *mirepoix*. Water and a roux are added. Seasoning is limited to a little black pepper and few dashes of Worcestershire sauce. There used to be no need of salt. Salinity came from the searing medium, rendered fatback pork. Salt pork fat is not for those with delicate digestion. I now, and this is admittedly rather poncy, use a heavy Greek olive oil with only enough salt pork to lend flavour, more a seasoning than a cooking medium. Bake, covered, for two hours.

Seal is said to be extremely good for you, high in this thing and that, low in other bad elements. I find it is restorative, has tonic properties, but put them down to the lift one gets from ritual, from a delicious seasonal meal, especially one of the spring, that puts you back in sync with cycles of the earth and the sea and of the family table. Like all the best of these seasonal feasts—lobsters, rabbits and partridge, turnip greens, capelin—you want a couple of feeds, that's all. There's no sense freezing them, no matter how well they keep, they don't taste right at the wrong time of year. Efforts to turn seal meat into something less strange to those from away, into sausage and such, have largely been failures.

Canned seal meat, for whatever reason, isn't very good at all.

There is little danger Sir Paul will ever stop the hunt, for his is a parasite-host relationship. Markets for the pelts have gotten better the past few years, fur is back in fashion as it will no doubt go back out. The appetite for seal meat in Newfoundland is still hearty, besides the home cooking there are plentiful church suppers and even takeaway preparations. But the taste will wane as the population continues to die off and emigrate. Unavailable in a President's Choice frozen "It's Too Good To Be True Newfie Soy-Flipper Pie" the children of the ex-pats will never develop a taste for the stuff and it will cease to be eaten by anyone but Arctic peoples until such time as their home and that of the seals melts away.

When Sir Paul gets the munchies he rifles the fridge for carrots and celery and papaya, for he is vegetarian.

NORDIC ENVY

I heard Jim Brown note last week what he took for a kind of Nordic envy in Canada, specifically a covetousness of things Danish. Canadians take the Danes as being similarly damp, cold and modest but somehow more successful at it. The Danes can figure out things, complicated things that still stump Canadians, like bike lanes and sex.

We have a variant of this sense of inadequacy here in Newfoundland and Labrador but it is in relation to things Norwegian. They are more like us than the Danes in that their economy is based on fish, oil and lumber. They like to eat stinky, salty seafood like us and are alcoholics. Their resource-based economy has made the Norwegians so rich they don't know what to do with their money. They can't even keep it all in Norway so have invested it the world over, effectively hedging their bets on tarry and fishy things. We in Newfoundland, with more oil and gas and fish and minerals and hydroelectricity, have somehow managed to arrange things in such a way that after harvesting those common resources to extinction we will remain destitute. Either the Norwegians really are smarter than us or we just love rapacious multinationals much more than they do.

So it really hurt when, last week, the lauded Norwegian novelist Karl Ove Knausgård visiting Newfoundland remarked, in a piece he'd written for the *New York Times*, that we were fat. Not just fat, but the fattest people he had ever seen. Not only the fattest he'd ever seen but utterly without compunction displaying our girth.

We in Newfoundland share with Canada a lingering colonial inferiority complex, so that crack, from a Norwegian no less, really stung. And there being no other local news that weekend other than someone using a drone to try to locate a lost dog, it got traction. On social media, Newfoundlanders took umbrage and tried to find something awful to say about Norwegians and coming up empty began wallowing in guilt and self-recrimination about the truth of the observation. We are fat. We loves a drop of Pepsi, we do! And fried things. And Jiggs Dinner. Mmmmm, Jigs Dinner.

There are plenty of Norwegians in Newfoundland now, they work for Statoil, the Norwegian State Oil Monopoly, since we in Canada are too dim to have fashioned such a thing to, you know, capitalize on all our own oil. They really are a very attractive people the Norwegians, so trim and fit and flaxen-haired you just wanna...squeeze them. But like Karl Ove they can be...dour? The myth that Scandinavians have the world's highest suicide rate persists because on meeting them it's easy to think, "Magnus is sure looking blue again today."

It's probably a kind of cultural misunderstanding, us taking the weak, forced smiles, the monotone voices and the literature and cinema as indicative of unhappiness when really it's something more lighthearted. Like when Max Von Sydow, who plays that fisherman in Bergman's *Winter Light*, a film that could have been set here in Newfoundland, and confesses to his Priest that he thinks life is meaningless...it's probably just the Nordic equivalent of "how's she goin', Fadder?"

Newfoundland and Labrador's Minister of Seniors, Wellness and Social Development (whatever that means) Clyde Jackman finally came out and acknowledged it. He said Karl had it, we're fat. He did so on the same day that the Member of Parliament for Nanaimo-Alberni in British Columbia, James Lunney, stated for the record that he didn't believe in evolution, climate change or vaccination and Alberta Premier Jim Prentice said his province was going broke. It's not the Danes or the Norwegians that are smarter than Canadians, it's every other population in the developed world.

MOUNT PEARL

It sure feels longer but Mount Pearl is sixty years old. As we celebrate the community's pithy history, exceptional snow clearing and elevator, it is interesting to note how few Pearlburghers can locate the mound that gives the municipality its name. And how many know that the promontory has yet to be scaled?

The first recorded attempt to "mount the Pearl" was by an expeditionary party of Sir Dudley Wigglingham, a widely despised contemporary of the more generally loathed Sir Humphry Gilbert, both uncles and cousins to the Queen and slayers of Irishmen. Arriving in St. John's harbour on the *Bark Auld Slut*, Sir Dudley—mad from knotty chromosomes and ergot rye mould in the ship's provisions—said he would claim the high land to the west in the name of Nancy. The remains of the crew, showing all the indications of having been cannibalized while still living, are buried beneath the tennis courts in Bowring Park.

More than a century passed before the pioneer adventurer, showman and self-styled Western Bayman Xavier King Cocksauce next attempted the hill. Given to fits of paranoia and a committed kleptomanian, the buckskin-clad King Cocksauce slipped away from camp under cover of darkness with all his team's horses. Those left behind stayed where they were to and established Goobies. King Cocksauce was forced to eat all of his mounts but one, Bess, which he married, never getting any closer to Mount Pearl than Paddy's Pond where his descendants still keep a barn.

Elwood MacPherson, the private secretary to Sir Richard Squires, was said headed to Mount Pearl with incriminating documents and a two-year supply of whiskey after fleeing the St. John's riot of April 5, 1932. Frequently disoriented, feeble-minded and only in office as a favour to his domineering father, the notorious bagman Boner MacPherson, Elwood got as far as a friend's country place in Topsail where, over an emotional long weekend of full-contact cronyism, he was put in various patronage positions.

During the Second World War the United States Air Force was to use Mount Pearl as a practice bombing target, even deeming it, in jest, Mount Pearl Harbour. The project was scrapped after the base commander at Fort Pepperrell absentmindedly doodled some racist cartoons of Newfoundlanders and African-American servicemen on the back of the top secret planning document.

The Lithuanian Inventor and static electricity visionary Paavo Lepmets was awarded seven million dollars by the Smallwood government in the hope of erecting a massive lint accumulation tower on the highest point of Mount Pearl. Fully charged the great shaft was to have made the entire northeast Avalon the only fully lint free jurisdiction in the world. But after cash payment for the project was delivered to a Munich address, Lepmets disappeared.

Persons wishing to climb it are urged to exercise extreme caution and to contact the City of St. John's for the appropriate permits for, as with most things interesting about Mount Pearl, the hill itself is actually within the boundaries of the capital city.

Originally published as "The History of Mount Pearl Like You've Never Heard It" in *The Overcast*, February 9, 2015.

NOTIONAL PUNCHEON

When local real-estate mogul Charlie Oliver announced that, instead of running for the Tory leadership, he was going to sponsor a think tank to tackle the intractable problems facing Newfoundland and Labrador, some joked a barrel was a more apt vessel in which to ferment local ideas. Certainly, to meet Heritage guidelines, the container should be made of wood. Rather than a National Think Tank we need a Notional Puncheon.

It's a capital idea. Boom or no we remain a tiny and isolated population. It's difficult to float challenging ideas in so small and close-knit a community. Say things people don't want to hear and you will come face to face with someone you've offended within the week. You don't anymore hear the expression "Wouldn't say 'shit' if his mouth was full of it" because it's sort of a self-fulfilling prophecy. Having a Notional Puncheon increases the odds of getting bad news before it's too late.

So I provide a short list of things that you cannot say in town as inaugural talking points for the institute or tank or tub or whatever it ends up being called.

- The future price of commodities (including energy) cannot be predicted with accuracy.
- Despite ceaseless crowing to the contrary, Newfoundlanders don't actually much care for and so do not in any meaningful way support their own arts and culture.
- A solution to both the unfunded pension liability and the skyrocketing cost of health care is to have people die sooner by denying them life-extending care at some threshold age.
- A significant cause of soaring health care costs is profiteering.
- It's not viable to provide ferry service to everyone who wants it.

- As we come to define the nation as a place to conduct business (as opposed to a place where we are citizens), corporate taxation has to contribute much more than 8% to the revenue side.
- Asphalt does not work as a road surfacing material in our climate.
- Big Oil owns and/or influences many politicians and most news media in Canada.
- MBAS make a company more profitable, less fun and shorter lived.
- There's a surfeit of hockey.
- Few defenders of CBC television can actually bear to watch it.
- How is it Newfoundlanders are so self-congratulatory and yet in constant need of approbation from the crowd on the mainland?
- Forget Blackouts '94 and 2014, the real worry is Starve-Out 20XX as we only have a seven-day food supply on the island.
- St. John's City Council doesn't grasp some central concepts of urban development because some members are too stunned.

The vessel is going to have to be enormous to accommodate the deep thinking required to address our problems. I doubt we any longer have the coopers capable of fashioning such a thing from staves. Maybe it should be made of reinforced fibreglass or some newfangled composite. The way things have been going we'll end up buying a used think tank from a Scandinavian country and shipping it over here, then find it only accepts Danish ideas.

A LITTLE KNOWLEDGE

Seeing that our low margin, boom and bust commodity-based economy is in the long nadir or deep, lightless trench phase of the cycle, we here at Newfoundland Eddicorp are pursuing opportunities in our little knowledge-based economy. And where better to begin that adventure than right here at home, with self-knowledge.

We've developed the Fib-bit, a wearable device that records the quotidian self-delusion of the client. At the end of the day, users simply upload the collected data, review the lies they've told themselves since waking and then take steps to, in the future, better face the facts.

Early results from trials here in town are encouraging. What follows is a recent sample of some of the auto-misinformation collected from twenty-three randomly selected St. John's men and women, ranging in age from 18 to 67, 19 times out of 20.

- Frank will grow as a human being and then we can seriously consider marriage.
- Eventually Rabbittown will be gentrified.
- Soon it will be spring.
- No one on the current city council is so blind they'd even consider running again.
- No strings attached.
- It's social drinking if you are messaging.
- I'm sure it's nothing.
- Shoulder season.
- The future price of oil.
- The bank has our best interest at heart.
- I needs a bigger truck.
- He's from Toronto but he gets it.
- It's pretty good hockey.
- Must be almost over.
- I'll take this work home and finish it tonight.

- Anything good on CBC?
- The Liberals just cannot be as bad as the Tories were.
- It is such a great idea, I'm sure I'll get the grant.
- This is probably a good time to shoot up to Costco.
- The Convention Center won't look like that when it's finished.
- Just for the one pint.
- Shag it, I'll have just one more.
- Sure she's crazy but she's not like "crazy" crazy.
- This is slimming.
- It's not really stealing if it's on the internet.
- Nobody is that stupid.
- Gonna start using public transit.
- There must be a reasonable bus route to work and back.
- Women love it.
- Bet they all think it was Brad who farted.
- If we behave as though things are as they used to be, things will return to being as they were.

Most promising is that these results were judged experimentally sound, being reliably repeatable day after day after day.

The fib-bit comes with a lifetime warranty.

Originally published as "The Fib-Bit: For Measuring Self-Delusion in St. John's" in *The Overcast*, February 29, 2016.

SEE MY BLOG

When I was there, things were done differently. It was all top people then, great bunch of guys, mostly Bonavista or Placentia baymen, best time in Newfoundland and Labrador. When I left the organization I was in possession of the kind of knowledge that can only come from experience, so I naturally assumed I'd be consulted by the new kids, at least for the big projects. Since I was on a generous pension I'd only charge standard consultancy fees, nothing like what we were paying Ernst and Young and SNC-Lavalin last going off—something reasonable, no more than $2000/day, something nominal.

Bastards never called. I never even got so much as an invite to the Christmas party, like I hadn't worked there for thirty-plus years! No surprise that it's all gone to shit. In my next blog post I will provide a series of graphs that demonstrate how Newfoundland and Labrador is now inexorably headed for bankruptcy and ruin regardless of any measures taken by any of the new people irrespective of any unforeseen future prospects. Further, my former colleague (retired) will offer evidence that in the past we did better things more often for much less.

You came up through the ranks, in my time, started at the bottom and learned how the whole operation worked. I started in the sub-basement, literally in the sub-basement repairing a sump pump. Wouldn't see a young executive doing that now! They don't teach you about sump pumps in Business School!

Here's a picture of me and the boys when the then-Premier knew my name and I was on that very important committee. Here we all are at the Chateau Laurier after we signed that breakthrough agreement with the Federal Government. They don't do agreements like that anymore. That agreement was the best ever negotiated by Newfoundlanders in Ottawa. Look at the hair! And look at the specs on my former assistant (retired)! We might have looked foolish but we got 'er done, buddy.

Back in the day they paid commentators to go on CBC. And that was when the CBC even had writers on contract! The only reason I do it for free now is because I have a pension that's pretty generous and the people of this once-great Province need to know that the new crowd have no idea how it's done. And at least CBC asks! Besides I'm up early in the morning, so it's nothing for me to drive to the studio, even from the cabin.

Our economists had a better grasp of the situation. Like us they started at the bottom, counting actual things, like cod tongues or birch junks, before they got into these theoretical projections.

Myself and my former colleagues (retired) were appointed strictly on merit. Our party affiliation was entirely coincidental to our being put in our posts. The new guys are the worst kind of cronies from the other party.

You would never get away with some of this stuff when I was there. Standards were higher then.

Originally published as "Blog Posts" in *The Overcast*, August 30, 2016.

BEST IN SHOW

I presume use of "on a go-forward basis" declined as we began slipping and then freefalling backwards. Ministers of the Crown or City Councillors can't very well go before the microphones saying, instead, "we'll consult stakeholders on a 'plunging-to-our-death' basis" or "on an inclusive 'Davy Jones'-locker-for-us-all' basis."

The new catch-all buzz phrase is "best practices." Apparently we are going to start adopting these. That we have been doing otherwise all these years is as hard to fathom as it is easy to see. For a number of reasons—routine corruption, endemic cronyism, anti-intellectualism, just plain pigheadedness—we've long employed "expedient practices," "spurious practices" and, perhaps most destructively, "usual practices." For a long time it was the usual practice here to turn a blind eye to certain "unnatural practices."

"Best" is a fuzzy word too, isn't it? It's a qualitative assessment, not unlike "nice." No one is boldly announcing we are moving to a rigorous new regime of "tested" or "most rational" practices. We should be stinking rich but are purportedly confronting hysterical "bankruptcy." I think by any measure if we were looking for the most successful state management of common natural resources we'd have to consider Norway's. But their methods aren't "best" for us because…well, I'm not sure why they aren't. When the brainless Bull Terrier is awarded "Best in Show" over the clearly more winning Dachshund, how are we supposed to know that the latter reminded the judge of an ex-husband? One person's "best" can be another's "meh."

We could try "better practices" but that is even more a confession of past mistakes. "Better practices" would mean sacking the former practitioners and when was the last time a patronage appointment was let go for incompetence, laziness or insanity? We don't do that here. We favour takers over makers. (The appointing of political pals to juicy sinecures, our Newfienomenklatura, is actually a "worst practice," not because it's immoral, but because we pay twice, once in generous salary and then, more often than not, to clean up after them.)

Besides, who really wants the most qualified candidate for a position introduced into the workplace? They'll only raise standards and so increase expectations. It's canny, ambitious bastards who surround themselves with people brighter and more talented than themselves. That's not us.

Our backs are to the wall, but it's a new day and with some ways, like those of the current City Council, now identified as "cocked-up practices," we declare that we are going to start doing things right for a change. Not just, right, goddamn it, but "best"!

It's a lot to ask. If we stand up too fast we'll likely hit our heads or get dizzy and fall over. I suggest we might start slowly, take a more gradual approach to civic and national improvement. Let's begin with "not-as-misguided-as-before practices" or "not-utterly egregious practices" so that we have the best, or at least a better, okay...remotely possible... chance of success.

Originally published as "Best and Better Practices" in *The Overcast,* February 2, 2016.

MINDFUL

Five years ago, six days after landing in St. John's for work related to the offshore oil play, Frank Delory joined Moksha yoga in the hope of meeting a hot chick and did. Jackie was an enthusiast not only for downward dogs and sirisanas but for anything with a sort of Eastern enlightenment vibe. She introduced Frank to "mindfulness," a condition of self-awareness that now, the morning after doing rails off the flush box of a toilet in a bar on George Street and demanding extra ice in his Jameson in effort to stay hydrated, only made his hangover worse. Frank really didn't want to be "in the moment" when it was this yeasty and pregnant with regret.

There was too much not to consider about St. John's. The taxi taking Frank to the airport had stopped for road repairs being made to Portugal Cove Road. A backhoe was punching holes in long-awaited asphalt so recently applied that it was steaming. The flag person, a grandmother in hard hat and pyjama bottoms, was twirling her sign so that it spun wildly from "Slow" to "Stop." Contemplating jobs awarded to lowest bidders, in whose interest it was to do the worst possible job so as to have more work the sooner, did not lead to clarity of mind. Frank belched and tasted yesterday's supper of street meat.

Frank fell hard for Jackie and was so convinced the feeling was mutual that he took advantage of her visiting the rural outpost where she was born, in order to help her family resettle, to get a tattoo, her name written over the Pink, White and Green tricolour that someone told him was the "real flag of Newfoundland."

He premiered the tat over dinner at the Adelaide Oyster Bar. Jackie's scream was mercifully lost in the punishingly loud music they played there to arrest conversation. It was not a shriek of surprise. It was of horror. Admittedly the tattoo was a bit of a rush job. But Jackie hadn't reacted to the unfortunate choice of script or ink, but because Frank had gotten it all wrong. Jackie thought they were great friends, special friends even, but nothing more. And what was with the weirdo Irish flag? Her family, she told him, were of English descent.

Next day, with the price of oil plummeting, the project to which he was assigned was put on hold and he was called back to Calgary. Someone said not to worry as the Saudis were going to run out by 2030. A day later he was informed the Calgary office was also being shuttered and his new destination was Houston.

The crazy Newfies at the St. John's office had thrown him the going away party and he'd only had time to rush back to the apartment and grab his bags with the taxi waiting outside. He didn't have a chance to go online and check to see if the flight was on time and was too out-of-it to be mindful of how foggy it was.

Air Canada told him it could be days before he could get another. Rather than go back downtown Frank checked into the Airport Inn to await the next flight out.

Originally published in *The Overcast*, September 28, 2015.

WATER
ON THE
BRAIN

It's heartening to see the City consulting with the public about what to do during and after the great tear up of Water Street. People are calling it "The Big Dig" after that massive infrastructure project undertaken in Boston to bury roads and green the place up. As it stands we are merely rooting out some old sewage pipes, replacing them and covering them back over, so our scheme is probably better described as "The Frig Dig." There have been a number of intriguing alternatives to the status quo presented—pedestrianizing the street or parts of it and so on—but my favourites look like they are going to be ignored.

1. Escape Tunnel: Danny Dumaresque's notion to use the dig as an opportunity to begin tunnelling to Europe to escape from the ever more deranged Canadians gets top ranking conceptually, but I am uncertain whether it's affordable at the rates Danny is charging to manage the project.

2. Totally Parking: A parking theme park, eliminating through-traffic and replacing it with a celebration of different styles of parking—lots, garages, towers, on street and off—seems appropriate but begs the question how one will drive to get there.

3. Heritage Graveyard: The remains of the built heritage we destroy could be dumped into the open ground so that archeologists from a future civilization could appreciate what we do not.

4. 'igh Line: This concept, a reclaimed elevated rail line celebrating our surrender of the train and veneration of the automobile, mimics a successful model in New York

City. But there are concerns that, being narrow gauge, it will not be wide enough and amblers may fall off the edge into the trench below.

5. Crony Hole: The last hire or appointment on merit in Newfoundland and Labrador was made, by accident, in Bay L'Argent in 1976. If and when it all comes crashing down thousands of political cronies will be in need of a bunker (and a vault) to hide from the torch mobs.

6. Beer Pit: Sort of an ultra-George Street; a pit, knee deep in sick, where drunken yomyocks could go to beat one another senseless for the amusement of onlooking crowds. Tourists will love this.

7. Municipal Chamber of Secrets: An underground bunker in which City Council can meet, clandestinely, to make decisions that contravene existing municipal guidelines.

8. Velodrome: I mean, bike lanes, fuck 'em right? Where do we think we are living? In the 21st century or something? "Park Free or Die!" All those who insist on peddling bikes about town could go around in circles literally, as well as figuratively.

9. Moat: Turning Water Street into a protective moat is probably the proposal with the greatest chance of success. The price is right, we just dig the trench and it floods itself. And it's necessary as tests of the harbour fence demonstrate that it can be hauled down by only six of Saladin's horses when the Muslim hoards attack.

Originally published as "Water (Street) on the Brain: 9 More Ideas Worthy of Consideration" in *The Overcast*, November 3, 2015.

DEAR CANADA...
SIGNED,
NEWFOUNDLAND

ear Canada,

It's been a while. I've tried calling but you won't pick up. I don't understand where things went wrong between us.

I know you've got a boatload of problems and are under a lot of stress. Anyway, I'm offering an old-fashioned letter instead, hoping you don't pitch it in the shredder unopened.

I'm writing to say that I appreciate what you are going through. You went all-in on the tar sands and it looks now like it was a bad bet.

I've been there. I once put it all on fish. I placed side-bets on timber and minerals. And I lost. And given a chance to fix the fishery I went and cocked it up again. Then you took over responsibility for the fishery and you cocked it up. Shit happens. I went double or nothing on offshore oil and now, as I write, they're towing my shiny new Dodge Ram Laramie Longhorn from the driveway. I didn't even need a truck!

You were once "the best country in the world" and "paragon of nations" and now you're a carbon pariah, exporter of asbestos to the third world, broker of arms to Saudi Arabian lunatics, the only industrialized country without door-to-door mail delivery or a public broadcaster.

You were once considered progressive and now you stand against arts and science. You decided empiricism was wrong, that's your choice, let the world laugh. The only friend you've got left is Israel and you're fine with that because you've decided you aren't going out any more, you're happy to stay home out of it.

Anxiety about your housing bubble is keeping you up nights. Listen, the royalty deal I cut with the resource multinationals starts my guts to boiling every time I close my eyes.

You're thinking now that NAFTA maybe wasn't such a good deal in the long haul but you bought into that neoliberal magical thinking thing so you're sort of obliged to see it through. I feel that way about Confederation once a week. But I'm Canada's Happy Province, so you know what? I grin and bear it.

You were taken over by creeps and thieves. Hey, I lost my national Government that way. I know how it can happen. And think about this, if the corruption endemic in my state hadn't destroyed it, you and I would still only be neighbours instead of... well...whatever it is that we are now.

You're hurting because you got shafted. Here's what I want to say to you: you are allowed to be angry. This act you put on; this polite, hockey-loving, good-natured-jokes-only, I-Am-Canadian, Tim Horton's swilling face you are showing to the world, everyone can see it's a mask. Those are bikers, Meth-heads and evangelical Christian nutters in the Ontario rust belt, not autoworkers and apple farmers. Stop saying you're sorry, go ahead and say you're pissed-off.

Let it go, Canada. Get past this bad patch and regroup. There nothing stopping you from making a clean start. You know where I am. Call me if you feel like going out for a drink or something.

Signed,
Newfoundland

Originally published in *The Overcast*, July 30, 2015.

GHOSTS OF CONFEDERATION

INT. WELL-APPOINTED LATE NINETEENTH CENTURY OFFICE IN OTTAWA. PURGATORY

The ghost of SIR JOHN A. MACDONALD walks to a credenza and pours himself a whiskey from a decanter. He takes a drink, but his form being insubstantial, the fluid just pours to the carpet. He sighs and puts the glass back down. The ghost of THOMAS D'ARCY McGEE enters, a bullet hole in his head. Sir John is startled.

McGEE
Sorry, John. Did I give you a start?

SIR JOHN
Almost a hundred and fifty years and I still
can't get used to that hole in your head.

McGEE
Reminds me, how are you feeling about the
sesquicentennial thing?

SIR JOHN
Honestly, being front and center for all
those years, *the* Father of Confederation,
was getting tired. But everyone has an
ego. Seeing myself in those Heritage
Minutes, on the ten-dollar bill, in "The
National Dream," I won't deny being
flattered.

McGEE
Feels odd to me, being left out of the story
this time.

SIR JOHN
Listen, D'Arcy, I thought the patriarchy and
colonialism were good things.

McGEE
"British" colonialism.

SIR JOHN
Accept no substitute. We did it best.

McGEE
Who is…I dunno…"replacing us" in the story?

SIR JOHN
A red couch.

McGEE
I don't understand.

SIR JOHN
Neither do I.

The door to the room flies open, the ghost of HECTOR LOUIS LANGEVIN storms in.

LANGEVIN
How dare they! How dare they!

McGEE
What is it this time, Langevin?

LANGEVIN
Not enough they took my name off that
bridge, now they are proposing it be taken
off "The Langevin Block."

SIR JOHN
I bet most Canadians who've heard "The
Langevin Block" on the news never ever
think to ask, "Who's Langevin?"

LANGEVIN
It's an outrage! After everything I gave to
Canada.

D'Arcy McGee points at the bullet hole in his head.

McGEE
Hector, need I remind you—

LANGEVIN
Yes, yes…you were assassinated, you're the
real martyr of Confederation, we know.

> McGEE
>
> Hector, dude, you had a central role in the formation of Residential Schools. Having your name taken off an old stone pile is getting off easy.

> LANGEVIN
>
> My actions have to be understood in terms of their historical context.

Sir John and McGee laugh at this.

> LANGEVIN
>
> What's so funny about that?

> SIR JOHN
>
> Only ghosts can understand things in their historical context, Hector, only ghosts.

> LANGEVIN
>
> God, McGee, that bullet hole in your head is a fright. Can't you wear a hat?

Sir John retrieves and dons a coat.

SIR JOHN

You Gentlemen can stay, but I have an appointment with Laurier.

LANGEVIN

Be careful.

SIR JOHN

Why?

LANGEVIN

Riel's about.

Sir John pauses, considers this news and then takes the coat back off.

SIR. JOHN

I'll see Laurier another day.

Originally published in *The Overcast*, April 3, 2017.

SESQUI
CENTENNIAL
ISMS

MEMO

From: Marie Vachon, Special Advisor 2nd
        Mandate Affairs, Prime Minister's Office

To: Sophie Trembly, Canada 150 Coordination,
        Heritage Canada

Re: Brand 150, Symbols

The 150th anniversary of Confederation is upon us so we have to consider what national symbols the Government can lever to extend its "honeymoon" with the electorate. Recent economic numbers pose risks to our standing so we have to seize this opportunity to keep the party going. The CPC gong show and NDP's existential crisis cannot make us complacent. The US election taught us that unemployed and underemployed voters can go crazy and consider voting against the establishment candidate, a troubling thought for "The Natural Governing Party."

We've burnt through iconic images in the early days of Sunny Ways to a degree that many can't be used again anytime soon. We've seen the Prime Minister in a canoe so often now that there are worries that the image could become a joke (see August 14 memo concerning the Prime Minister going shirtless).

The Beaver, a once reliable symbol of Canada's beginnings, is really about the fur trade. Might as well celebrate the seal hunt if you think about it. Besides, it's a big rodent. How do we feel about Moose?

Market research tells us the first association most Canadians have with the Maple Leaf is Toronto's hapless hockey team so it is strictly out of contention.

Further to Canada's national game, former PM Harper appropriated hockey with enough success that there are lingering associations. We also don't want to risk pointing out that the NHL is an American entertainment business run out of New York. And Gary Bettman would fleece us for the rights.

Cowboy hats remind Albertans of guys from Ontario that ran the place for the oil companies and left it a smouldering ruin.

Anything to do with our colonized and marginalized aboriginal people smacks of cultural appropriation (see July 2 memo regarding Prime Minister's tattoo) and is to be avoided at all costs. Needless to say they won't be celebrating with us.

Steer clear of Maritime-themed stuff like lobsters and lighthouses while we are in the process of stripping the Atlantic Provinces of power within the Confederation. Newfoundland and Labrador hasn't been with us for the full 150 and most of their symbols are already clichés locally so we can, thankfully, continue to pretend they don't exist.

Especially with rumblings of NAFTA indigestion coming from south of the border we really have to celebrate Canada having lower taxes on business than almost any jurisdiction in the G20. Really cheap consumer goods made in Mexico and China do make our nation great.

Quebec blackmailing the rest of country is a generally known condition but it's difficult to imagine a family-friendly image representing it.

Massive pipelines using billions of gallons of freshwater to force tarry sludge to the United States is very Canadian but we can't see any interesting ways of representing it graphically.

The most positive associations for Canada during audience testing came when sample groups were shown an image of Donald Trump, but marketing Canada as not being the United States is fraught with problems.

Poutine is safe. Poutine we like. Thoughts?

Originally published as "Memo, Re: Brand 150 Symbols" in *The Overcast*, January 9, 2017.

CHATTER BOXES

If texting predated the phone, people would abandon their handheld devices the moment a chubby Bakelite rotary dialler was in reach. "Have you tried phoning? It's like texting only you actually speak to the person! So much faster! And it's amazing, you get all this nuance. Turns out Ed was being sarcastic!"

Texting is primarily a way of avoiding, not making, contact. Text recipients glance at their expensive phones (originally designed to be used as phones) mostly to see to whom it is they are not replying. The content of the message is secondary to being acknowledged by someone you refuse to acknowledge. It's Cartesian one-upmanship.

The same people who ignore messages are outraged when their own go unanswered. "I've been texting and texting him! What can he possibly be doing?"

Most texts are so peremptory and garbled, the equivalent of grunts and snorts, as to require clarification in the form of a more carefully thumb-typed follow-up text.

I've yet to meet anyone who needs "unlimited texting" because they have a lot to say.

If you have to resort to emojis to make the meaning of your words clear, you should probably read more and get the hang of English. Emojis are cave drawings that someone else had to create for you because you aren't so good with a pointy stick. And they had more class at Lascaux than to give a bad review of the hunt by sketching a steaming pile of ibex poop.

Email has fallen out of favour because it's on the record and demands finished thoughts and complete sentences. When people try to read an email of any length and substance on their phone, they invariably only scan it and get upset about something they misread. Then they'll text you back.

In a bizarre turn, Skype afforded us a live picture of the person we were speaking with, after texting rudeness was already widespread in the population. People with ADHD attention spans are perfectly willing to stream you their waning interest. They will fiddle with stuff on their desk, look at and react to other windows open on the screen and, as though you were not looking straight into that room *at them*, start signalling and mouthing messages to people off camera.

Just because privacy is outmoded doesn't mean you have license to share everything.

Business has learned to capitalize on the decline in meaningful communication by developing algorithms which make buying easier and return nearly impossible. Call volumes are always higher than normal so you will always wait long enough that most suckers will simply give up. You can buy a plane ticket in an instant but it takes you an afternoon to change it.

It's difficult to get much done via a website if you are required to change passwords and PINs more frequently than you use it. The system at

MUN is comically cumbersome and clunky in this respect—it's like someone from the Computer Science Department built it.

Going somewhere to meet in person lets you use and read body language, you feel humanity. It gets you out of your bubble and blows a little stink off. Use your smartphone for what it does best, selfies and Pokémon GO. The most effective way to communicate is face to face. JS.

Originally published as "Chatterboxing Ourselves In" in *The Overcast*, August 4, 2016.

MARCH

After one hundred and twelve freeze/thaw/ freeze/freeze cycles, the woods road brandished a carapace of diamantine ice nearly a foot thick. On my way in with the dog, there was freezing rain that turned, briefly, to rain, before another transition into needles. Coming back out, I found myself on a hill, a steep bank of snow at my back, the road-surface ice on ice now water-covered and as slippery as motor oil. I couldn't take a step down or up without going off on my arse and likely breaking or blowing something. Would I have to crawl back to the car, the dog barking at me to get back up on two legs like a proper biped? "Why are you freaking me out?" she would yip. Would I actually be reduced to getting down on my hands and knees, like a penitent, to move forward? Why would anyone live here? I imagined selling everything at the bottom of the market and moving to a tiny stone hut in the South of France. But my wife won't accept hut living. The best option was clearly to lie down and die. I'd be found once the snow melted in July.

Two days later, after a modest snowfall, I was in the country again. The sky was a deep daytime blue, stretching to cobalt, bluer than any sky I'd ever seen. The sun, reflected from the fresh snow, was putting charge in the glister coating the trees, so even in the brilliant daylight, every branch seemed illuminated. The air was clean. The only sound was the tinkling of icy limbs and a crow at a distance. The dog was bounding ahead to the next promontory just to strike a pose, so stunningly beautiful was the situation.

Maybe you're not bipolar, maybe it's Newfoundland.

The head doctor who identified Seasonal Affective Disorder did so in Maryland. At this latitude, on this perch out in the Labrador Current, it surely scales up to something like Seasonal Affective Raging Psychosis. It's Spring in Maryland now.

In the Rhone, with the stone huts of my dreams, they speak of the Mistral, a wind funnelled in the river valley that is at times so ceaseless it drives men mad. Imagine, "ceaseless wind." The Mistral is powerful enough to blow lawn furniture into swimming pools. What then can be the state of mind of the semi driver whose rig has been lifted off the highway in the Wreckhouse and tossed into the tuckamore? What comes after madness?

Back in the day, when pirates would crowd into The Ship Inn to self-medicate, you could bring your dog as long as it was well behaved and would sit under the table. By March, the seasonal cocktail of cabin fever, cold and damp, the drink, and the end of unemployment insurance could dangerously darken the mood of that beer parlour. Relationships ill-fated from the start, whether with a lover or other cast members, rarely stood the strain. The swords we all thought kitschy ornaments came off the wall once. "Jaysus, they're real swords," everyone thought, wondering who would be killed.

It's April. You live in Newfoundland and you've made it. You have demonstrated an emotional fortitude unknown anywhere else desperate settlers have built a tilt. You are a victorious soldier of the psyche, tough enough to go back to the field of battle and rescue your wounded comrades. Despite a few tears along the way, you have survived. You're tough enough to laugh. Congratulations.

SO GO STORIES

A lot of "tradition" is recent invention. Kilts and tartans are quite late to the Scottish Highlands. Chicken Tikka Masala is such a delicious British concoction it's ended up on menus in India. Tin whistles are English, originating in Manchester in the 1840s.

We're mad for making it up here. I recently saw "Screech-In" described as "traditional" in Government sponsored content. Not sure when that foolishness began but I never heard tell of such a thing before the 1980s. The "Pink, White and Green" is not an official flag of anything and the term "Republic of Newfoundland" was coined by a guy from Texas named "Snuffy." More recently there's the "Mummer's Parade" and the proposition that the colourful attached housing of the downtown is called "Jelly Bean Row." It's all made up and, really, what odds? A fifth of the population recently tried to pull a mass-Boyden and reinvent themselves as "Qalipu," that landless band itself another recent invention.

We don't so much suspend disbelief anymore, we drop it. Witness the profusion and persistence of "alternative facts." I put it down to the increasingly facile nature of the narratives we consume. People read less and watch more, making them passive recipients of story. And film and television stories are less and less sophisticated, a great many of them, even for grown-ups, featuring magic or superpowers. "Think pieces" have become scarce as print news media dies. There's no long, deep read in the weekend paper because no one will pay to have them written. Instead you scan decontextualized tweets on your phone as you hate-drive the Outer Ring Road at 150 km/h. Our diet has dulled our critical faculties to the point we don't know what to believe, so we believe anything.

And we all believe what we want to believe. I've often quoted the Churchill chestnut, "Then what are we fighting for?" explaining why he wouldn't cut arts funding during the war effort. I learned recently that he never said it.

In fiction we go in for protagonists with whom we can effortlessly identify. We demand redemptive endings. We reject characters with ambiguous motives and stories with open endings. We want our belief systems reaffirmed not challenged. We want the tale to reassure us. Thus "Make America Great Again" was more effective than the Clinton slogan you can't remember.

The one cringe-worthy piece of storytelling in Citizen Kane, "Rosebud" has come to define it. The scene tells you, "Kane's last real happiness was that moment, in childhood, with his sled." The ending of *The Sopranos* television series, a black-out into permanent anxiety, was decried as a betrayal but it better reflected reality and made you wonder.

Of course "Rosebud" was actually mischief by screenwriter Herman Mankiewicz who knew it to be a pet name William Randolph Hearst had for a corner of his mistress's Marion Davies' anatomy.

Or so the story goes.

A traditional Qalipu ceremony is every bit as legit as the Lieutenant Governor (representing the

House of Saxe-Coburg and the magical authority of Divine Right) being piped to the head table by a guy in a skirt and tall feather bonnet. That you possess Irish or Nova Scotian Mi'kmaq or Basque deoxyribonucleic acid, that your ancestors were of the homicidal Bay Roberts' Mummers, may mean a lot to you but it's backstory, it's the past. The more interesting part is yet to come.

XMAS

Christmas is, of course, nonsense. It's the co-opting of the Romans' Saturnalia by the early western Christian church. The Aramaic speaking Palestinian freedom fighter whose birth it celebrates most likely came into this world in the late summer or early fall, not around December 25th, and probably four years earlier than once supposed. That's if he existed at all.

Not so long ago I visited an early Orthodox Christian church in south eastern Bulgaria, near the Turkish border, and that faith's oriental character is quite at odds with the blanched Protestant expressions around which I grew up. Playing with Catlick youngsters who had ash unaccountably smeared on their foreheads was as exotic as things got on Ennis Avenue.

Who cares, the contemporary Christian West worships a fictive, vaguely Italianate gay-porn Jesus in the diaper, not some dark skinned Middle Eastern terrorist type. I'm not a believer and loathe the commercialism but, having lived most of my life in town, adore Christmas because St. John's does it so well.

The downtown of St. John's has the right look, with snowy accents like those of black and white movie Victoriana. If a window opened and Alastair Sim appeared to bid some corner boy buy him a turkey at Halliday's you wouldn't look twice. The crowds hurrying about in their woolly hats and mittens, trailing plumes of breath, remain as willing as they ever did to stop and talk. And our St. John's setting is boreal, the city is nestled in a forest of Tannenbaum. The South Side hills are like a great wreath over the harbour. Christmas in a warm place is just another holiday.

Townies still bother to hang plenty of lights and decorations. The late December days are the darkest of the year so there is wisdom is this. It's more than cheerful, it's a prophylactic measure against the seasonal affective disorder that plagues so many people in these latitudes.

In keeping with the Saturnalian roots of the festival there is still a taste in town for feasting, singing, drinking, for all variety of merrymaking. Conviviality is, blessedly, still a thing in our remote and foggy outpost. I know and enjoy the company of my neighbours and we will all, through the season, get together for a few drinks and stories. That's really something for which to be thankful.

We must make our toasts this year in the context of tables overturned and blood spilled in Paris. Innocents there were targeted because they had congregated in bistros to enjoy food and wine in the company of friends or to join in watching a band. They had as little to do with France's colonial legacy and the imperial crimes of the West as Syrian refugees have to do with Salafist inspired terror. Our greatest gift this Christmas is to be able to celebrate and argue and love and believe or not believe in any religious foolishness or flags in peace.

Resist intolerance and thuggery by keeping the "Merry" in Merry Christmas. Joyeux Noël. Vive la France.

Originally published as "Christmas is Nonsense; Christmas in Town is Quite Nice" in *The Overcast*, December 5, 2015.

TREES

A mature tree in the city is a success, a great idea realized. If someone planted it they have all our blessing. If it was a volunteer we cheer the tree's own enterprise.

Large deciduous trees are forgiven their vanity because it is deserved. Horse Chestnuts around St. John's are for most of the year stolid, graceless things, but when they put on flowers and exaggerate their architecture you concede their magnificence. Their perfume is subtle. The fruit, that spiny green medieval mace is ridiculous but Horse Chestnuts get away with it just as some people can get away with smoking a pipe. And conkers is to The Higher Levels as fencing is to Montparnasse.

Lilacs live across the street for years and you consider them bent and old and pitiable until one day in June when they get dolled up and take a much younger lover. Lilacs are floozies.

Maples are Canadian weeds and unwelcome.

Laburnum or Golden Chain is difficult to cultivate in most locales. It wants a particular acidic soil and an admixture of general climatic dreariness and gallows humour such as is found on The Avalon. The English covet and struggle to grow them but they do not have, despite all their palaver about London "pea soupers," an adequate understanding of fog-based silviculture.

There is no need to expand on how Birches are the most literary of trees.

Flowering crabs are the wooded world's thespians; so alluring during the show that you fall for them only to discover later, after they've brought over a toothbrush and a change of clothes, that they were only *playing* an apple.

Beeches are well put together, fit and tall with perfect posture. Copper Beeches the same, only in bespoke. Hedged Beeches are East End chauvinists. They are the hardest working trees and so held in surprisingly high regard by their towering brethren.

I have a Siberian Elm on my lot with so thick an accent it is all but incomprehensible to the other trees on the street. And it doesn't care.

Coniferous trees have their own story. Native spruce and fir are as comfortable in town as most baymen. They dream of ponds and bogs. They find the term "urban forest" as pretentious as planting an "s" in the middle of Georgetown. Native pine no longer so heavily clad our hills because, having been proven right about Confederation, they've stopped caring. Imported, nursery-bought pines are like someone from New Brunswick trying to be witty at a dinner party—i.e. better not to. Larches, with several aliases, are unusually nervous for a conifer and are probably up to no good.

The essential townie tree, the corner boy of trees is, or course, the Dogberry; scraggly, unkempt, showing some garish flash in daring to wear that hue of orange, tending to show up uninvited.

Trees have lately deliberated on the issue and while they agree being anthropomorphized as they are here is wrong, they relish being talked about and admired.

Plant one.

Originally published as "Townie Trees" in *The Overcast*, April 2014.

SOLVITUR AMBULANDO

In the same week I heard on the radio that the key to health was, "owning a dog and a good pair of walking shoes," an old pal, his middle age heft increasing, reported being prescribed a hound by his family doctor.

That walking, more than a diet of mashed flax and booboo berries or twelve hours a week at the gym on the glute-jammer, is the key to health and that a restless mutt in the house is one of the few things that will guarantee you'll do so should be news to no one. Less understood is how a dog will show you *how* a walk is properly done and further, if you heed its canine ways, how your mental health will improve as much as your cardiovascular prospects with each step you take.

The first lesson is that every walk, even along a commonly trodden way, is new. In fact, monitoring the subtle changes in a daily route can be more meditative than breaking new trail. Dogs never tire of the same route because it is never the same walk.

The walk itself should be everything, done for its own sake, not for exercise, not out of obligation and definitely never to get somewhere. That you might have a destination is not a concern, but needing one doesn't work. The experience is about what you take in: simple sights, sounds and smells. Walking in company is fine and conversation (the quality of which is improved by perambulation) is no hazard. But nothing will sort your head quite like a stroll with only your dog for company.

Checking your phone is pretty much the only thing that can completely and irretrievably shag up a good walk. If you're going to fixate on your devices you might as well be home in your pyjamas as out in the country.

The matter of "a good pair of walking shoes" is complicated on the Avalon.

You require high rubber boots, "Bayman-Go-Fasters" we used to say, to contend with the muck and the melt-swollen brooks and the snow and slush. These are rarely comfortable or flattering. A tall and slender woman can look smart in leggings and a pair of Hunters but any doughy dude north of 20 years in rubber boots and track pants invariably has a "between gigs" aspect. You will, sometime in our beastly seasons, find yourself facing a path of water-covered ice as slick as motor oil and calculate you must crawl lest you go off on your arse. You need, as dogs demonstrate, claws on your footwear.

We are blessed in this foggy burgh with the urban pedestrian routes the Johnson Foundation restored and maintain and the genius of the East Coast Trail on our margins. Our air is clean, the views inspiring, few on earth have as many enchanting options afoot.

Diogenes The Cynic said, "it is solved by walking." Considering Newfoundland and Labrador's current cargo of mindbenders we should all be taking to shanks' mare. By other means we have a tendency to go in circles.

Originally published as "Walking the Dog" in *The Overcast*, June 2, 2017.

EVERLAND

e was scowling at his menu, not even bothering with a hello when I arrived. It had been years and years yet he carried on as if I'd just returned from the gents.

"Seared Tuna? Crikey. Do you know, Peter, there was once a grog house on this very spot. Brothel upstairs. They served a game pie, one with a fair measure of grouse in it...and you never see a pickled egg any more. I fancy the scattered pickled egg."

He made a show of reaching for a piece of bread.

"That's...new?" I ventured.

"Yes," he said, turning his good eye to the prosthesis. It was of a synthetic with a Pepto-Bismol hue, one poorly approximating flesh. "Took a bit of getting used to."

"I would have thought, practicality aside, the hook was…was?…*eponymous* isn't the right word, rather the reverse. Something of a trademark, at least."

"It had become a cliché, Peter. Truth be told, I was tiring of the act. One night, we were ashore in Madeira and this stunning wench…sorry, this *young woman*…had the gall to say I looked like 'Johnny channelling Keef.'"

"Better than Ratzo Rizzo."

"Or Mork," he answered after a moment.

"I can't stay long."

"No, I suppose not, banker's hours and all. I'll get right to it then. As I say I'm getting out of the racket and…well…I'm offering you the ship."

"The Roger?"

"Yes, and the Captaincy, of course. There's very little sailing or swashbuckling involved any longer. I licensed the thing to Disney ages ago. It's mostly public appearances now, no piracy at all, leastways of the old sort."

"I don't see how I could. This is very sudden."

"I know but what with this new book coming out and yet another pirate movie come Christmas….

And say what you will Peter, you're the natural choice. If you read between the lines it's terribly obvious that if you had stayed with us…."

"Yes, yes, yes, I've heard it all before."

"If I had a doubloon for every time someone told me that I had refused to grow up," he shook the false arm at me, "for every time some women evoked your name as I left her bed chamber. I may have been lapped by my own reference, but you've given name to a complex. What a legacy," he cackled.

"An unfair characterization, given the circumstances," said I.

"Indeed." He quieted, steadying to take aim. "How is Mrs. Pan, by the way?"

"Wendy…she's wonderful. Bit of a battle or a series of skirmishes, with depression. It's being treated."

"No more flying about the room, then?"

"One crashes."

"Yes she's better with her feet on the ground."

"There are still a lot of unresolved issues concerning her father, I'm afraid."

He didn't want to hear this and changed the subject.

"Tinker Bell is in town too, you know. She's still flying."

"Wendy doesn't even know I'm here, Hook. She wouldn't be very happy."

"Arrr…" he started and then, catching himself, made as though he was just clearing his throat. "Come on, join us, just for tonight, for old times' sake, we're going for a few ales, the Lost Boys too, we'll be going straight on 'til morning, Peter."

"I can't."

"No, I suppose not."

"Remember me to Miss Bell."

"That I will Peter, that I will. And best to Mrs. Pan."

SEEING YOU HERE

B lame force of habit, if you like, or early-on-set misanthropy or just the simple rules of coincidence: but none of this would ever have happened if she hadn't got up before dawn to beat the holiday traffic

Blame force of habit. Strong force. Being excessively "anticipatory" was an admitted flaw of Charlotte's. It was another of her traits that had, finally, driven Terrence away. It wasn't "over-eagerness" for she responded in the same fashion to things to which she looked forward as to those she dreaded. And it wasn't, as last going off Terrence characterized it, "obsessive compulsive."

She was always early. Charlotte was commonly so early for a plane or a train that she now routinely booked the earliest trip of the day. If she had a flight at three in the afternoon she would wake for it before dawn, she would have packed the night before, she would be out of the shower ahead of schedule, she would be at the airport and checked-in before a gate was assigned. Terrence was quite the opposite. Terrence could manage everything at the last minute and never be in a rush. His entire life went that way, walking from the airport limo to the check-in and directly on board, finding his seat, or being bumped to executive as a reward for his tardiness and winning smile, always buckling up just as the plane lurched from the bridge. Terrence was unflappable. Now, living by herself, with no one to keep her tendency to jump the gun in check, Charlotte was earlier and earlier still.

Last evening, with her Subaru gassed-up, with a bottle of water for the journey already in the fridge, with her loose teal cotton pants and ivory short-sleeved shirt laid out, with sunglasses clipped to the car's sun visor, with her efficient little overnight bag packed for every contingency (Terrence once called it her "bat bag" and she'd first mistook his meaning and there had been a cyclonic row), with all that done and beginning to fall into dreams she recalled the holiday. Revision of her plans, to begin the drive now before dawn, kept her up half what was left of the night. And the dreams did not come back.

These last months she dreamt richly and took a greater role in the making of these reveries than at any point in her life. The night shows were not so accidental as once they were. Being alone liberated the imagination and in the darkness of the bedroom she could just about cast and script them. Just about. They were teeming.

Misanthropy? No. Living by oneself at 46 years of age did not mean she didn't like people. And wasn't she going to spend the night at Hettie and Dave's cottage outside Chester? That was downright sociable. Though she wondered whether they made the invitation assuming she would decline. The rest of them would be couples. Maybe the invite had been a courtesy, or worse, a mercy.

The simple rules of coincidence were always, for Charlotte, rigorous. Today, leaving Halifax, she caught only green lights. She was the last car waved across the MacDonald Bridge by a traffic marshal before it was closed to allow for a mammoth tractor trailer with a wide load of concrete culverts to pass. Driving conditions were ideal. The day was balmy, the air relieved occasionally by a minty onshore breeze. There were sprays of cloud in the highest sky. There was, improbably, no road work being undertaken. By the simple and rigourous rules of coincidence she was making time. None of it would have happened if she hadn't got up before dawn to beat the holiday traffic.

"Drive out for drinks and dinner, there are a bunch of people coming and it's just beautiful down there now. Bring a bathing suit, the water's cold but if it's a hot day... Stay for supper and then spend the night, you can drive back the next day. You'll be able to relax that way, have a few glasses of wine."

Charlotte coaxed the names of the other guests from Hettie and, satisfied she wasn't being set up, as before, with some busted jazz musician or patently unbeddable Dalhousie economics professor, agreed to go. Julie and Henry were going, Otto and Elizabeth, old friends of hers and Terrence. No one would mention the split. Probably no one but Charlotte still thought of it now, two years after the fact. Though if Henry was spending the night he would doubtlessly have one or six too many G & Ts and—punchy from too much sun, his balding pate scorched—say something tactless. Hettie, too, could occasionally go off the rails and in saying anything at all, by statistical necessity, eventually say the wrong thing. Hettie put these manic episodes down to either hypo- or hyperglycemia, Charlotte couldn't remember which. Charlotte thought the cause was more likely a good old-fashion personality disorder than an issue of blood sugar. After accepting Hettie's invitation, Charlotte wondered if Terrence and the new wife, Nancy, hadn't already been guests and if Hettie was inviting her not out of pity, but out of guilt. If so it was entirely possible that Charlotte would sleep in the same bed, throw off the same sheets in the heat of the summer night as had her ex and his second Nancy. As always Terrence walked out the door and, without having to wait, walked straight into that relationship. Probably figured he'd been bumped-up once again, bumped-up through life.

She was already out of Dartmouth and on the highway.

All her and Terrence's friends had summer places on the South Shore, in and around Chester and Lunenburg and Mahone Bay and this, she only now realized, was her first invitation to any of them since the split. They were worried about having a weekend poisoned by her bitterness. Fair enough. You saw it all the time. Debbie, a colleague, was doing the sixteenth year of a self-imposed term of toxic rage. Charlotte was fine with her divorce, was even now finding a sort of contentment in being by herself, a serenity that wasn't expected, wasn't allowed a single woman. She knew that when she said such, that she was doing better than well, people didn't believe her. People thought they knew her better than she knew herself. They thought Charlotte was merely putting on a brave face. They wanted some crying on the inside. If Charlotte was unhappy, destroyed by loneliness, then they could rationalize their ever chillier second and third marriages.

She was ahead of the pack on the highway. She had risen early enough to have the road almost to herself. She felt inclined to wave to the occasional oncoming vehicle. She was going to be early. She turned on the radio.

It wouldn't do to arrive so long before the others, to be parked outside the cottage awaiting their arrival. How desperate would that look? She knew she should be beyond caring but…

Curious that she and Terrence were alone among their friends in not having a summer place on the Shore. Likely Terrence sensed, long before Charlotte, that their union wouldn't last and avoided acquiring another piece of matrimonial property that defied easy division.

She could already see the fog that seemed to permanently envelope the head of St. Margaret's Bay. Stewart and Linda had a place down there, in Hubbards. She considered a detour to drop by and see them, stop by for a coffee to kill some time. But the mist was uninviting and she would only be putting herself back on the highway in the worst of the getaway rush. She looked at the speedometer and, seeing she was driving 130 km/h, eased off on the gas.

The roadside ditches were filled with lupines and even with the windows rolled up, their pepper and soap scent was entering the car. Charlotte associated the smell, for some lost reason, with summer lightning. On the hills beyond they were farming Christmas trees, neatly groomed jade pyramids set apart like pieces on a board game. All that Yule in the heat of summer—it was like a child's fever, good memories undifferentiated, an entire landscape of holiday. Charlotte supposed working there might be like eating too many sweets.

She was hoping to hear the weather, hoping to plan too far ahead for the drive back, maybe finding an excuse to cut the visit short, having to beat the rain. But between numbing musical selections, the CBC radio program's congested host would not give a forecast. Instead he was issuing a stream of autobiographical banalities and doing so with all the vigour of stale air leaking from a flaccid balloon. Charlotte couldn't bear anymore and turned it off. It came to her that this was how she had heard the accusation of misanthropy; it had been Terrence, after she had complained about the dire condition of public radio one afternoon.

"It's just background, they're not trying to be fascinating, interesting even," Terrence had said. "You're asking too much of it, and way too much of the people doing it. Being dissatisfied with everyone all the time…it's misanthropic."

She looked in the rear view. A Volvo wagon that had been tailing her since Tantallon was taking the exit to Hubbards. In the corner of the mirror, before the world falling behind, she saw a portion of her temple and forehead, the font of the grey in her hair.

Charlotte considered that she was getting better looking, was better suited to this body than the one she inhabited in the years before. The few silvery hairs—and she was trying to be objective about this—actually seemed to make her younger, as if she was a "young 46" when she had been an "old 38." Living alone she discovered a vast reservoir of time. She was freed from the steady maintenance, like that on an old house, that a relationship demanded. In the surplus hours she was taking better care of herself. She fulfilled a resolution to strenuous daily exercise—gym, pool, the four kilometre walk to and from work—and felt tight and hard as a board. She sometimes caught herself, supine on the bed or the yoga mat, vainly testing the tension of lower belly, fingering new ridges of muscle. This first came with a pang, a want, a need to test it or prove it by another's touch, but now this desire was losing urgency.

Yes, "misanthropy" was unfair. Hasty judgment and minding other people's business was such a marked characteristic of the human species. What purpose did it serve? Pack animals, like dogs, nuzzling one another's haunches.

Exit 7, East Chester. It wasn't yet ten in the morning. No, none of it would have happened if she had not gotten up so early to beat the holiday traffic, to get ahead of that pack.

Her growing agitation at being early, again early, made the compact car smaller. Would she go into the town and shop? For what? Lobster pot and Bluenose tchotchkes, a golf shirt with "Chester" on the breast. From Ottawa originally, Charlotte had taken notice of the Nova Scotian's taste for golf shirts, and for those short pants with multiple pockets, the kind you might wear rock climbing. And hiking boots, even in Halifax, in the city, they wore hiking boots. This was their national costume. Terrence, a native, was in the bloody shorts from April until December despite the climate. The only concession they made to the cold and wet might be a sweater. The sweater and shorts combo was, Charlotte believed, a self-evident contradiction, a sartorial oxymoron. Charlotte was convinced that the local tribe were evolving to have permanently tanned knees. She had moved east following Terrence.

She saw Exit 8 to Chester ahead and decided to continue past, to go as far as Lunenburg, which she had never visited, for lunch, and then turn around and go back to Hettie's cottage when there was more likely to be someone there.

She knew that Lunenburg had a history of ship-building and, driving into town, Charlotte saw that the houses in the town were possessed of a strength that could be described as seaworthiness. It was as sturdy a place as it was smart. She parked in a public lot, license plates from all over.

Stepping from the car the air smelled of grease from a clam and chip stand in a converted school bus across the parking lot. There was what looked to be a pub across the street. Having been in the confines of the car and the day so hot, Charlotte set off in search of lighter fare.

The village center was pretty in an entirely false way. It had been completely converted to tourism. Clusters of sightseers moved on the sidewalks like grazing ruminants, slowly forward, heads down to the map and then up to confirm they were where they thought they were.

She possessed a visceral loathing for tourists even as she was one. True misanthropy would have to include self-loathing wouldn't it? What if Terrence was right about her?

She saw a small sandwich board on which were chalked daily specials. It stood before a lemon-coloured wooden building, a meticulously restored three-story Victorian affair. Charlotte decided to eat there without even reading what was on offer.

The momentum of the weighty door swinging inward carried and deposited her before a small lectern on which rested a wide book for reservations. She must have made a commotion, for standing and waiting there, she sensed she was being stared at.

The rooms were pleasant, grander than she expected. There were vases of sweet pea and zinnias on the cream linen table clothes. The settings were silver.

A trim young woman with a tight bun of auburn hair emerged from the swinging door at the end of wide hallway. Beyond the door Charlotte caught a brief glimpse of an unhurried kitchen.

"Hello."

"Hello. I don't have a reservation."

"That's fine," The young woman asked, unconsciously looking about for the rest of the party, "is someone joining you?"

"Oh just the one, just me," said Charlotte.

"I'm afraid there's nothing left on the patio."

"Inside is okay," said Charlotte.

The young woman beckoned Charlotte to follow.

Charlotte was seated in what must have once been the drawing room. There was an enormous fireplace on the rear wall. She declined anything to drink but a glass of water. The menu was interesting. It was a more serious restaurant than she'd thought. She decided on fresh mackerel with a tomato sauce (tomato sauce!), accompanied by a beet salad, only because it seemed so wrong, so out-of-a-tin, that she reasoned to be offered alongside local scallops and lamb and haddock, it must be special. The waitress commended her choice with an enthusiasm Charlotte took to be genuine.

Two of four other tables were occupied, both by couples, one elderly, the other about her age. Of this second couple she could only see the face of the man, with whom she made eye contact. He tried to hold her gaze for a moment as if he thought he knew her. Charlotte concluded that this man must have been the one looking at her as she had stood by the entrance.

Charlotte knew that a woman dining alone always got unbidden attention. And it was not, as one might expect, from men who were themselves alone that she most commonly drew looks. The movie scene, the dashing gent who, with a sweeping gesture of a sturdy hand to the unoccupied chair opposite, said, "Mind if I join you," never happened. No, the glances came not from men who were alone but from those who were already in the company of another woman.

Were they, Charlotte wondered, comparison shopping, measuring the woman they were with against her? Even if they were seemingly content, or in high spirits, smiling and garrulous at that moment, they couldn't help but wonder if they made the right decision in coming this far in life—be it a month or twelve years—with their Judy or Diane or Heather. Some surely had regrets. Did Terrence look over Charlotte's shoulder one meal and see Nancy?

The mackerel was spectacular. It was grilled and the flesh was more delicate and moist than any fish she had ever tasted. The sauce was of barely cooked fresh cherry tomatoes, bright acidity making it more a sort of pickle. The beet was in a tower with goat cheese mortar and rested in a pool of emerald oil, volatile with basil.

The man at the other table watched her eat the meal like his head was invisibly tethered to her fork. Charlotte could feel his gaze. She wished to be left alone and, once finished, impatiently flagged the waitress with her credit card.

There was a stigma to eating by oneself, again that whiff of desperation. There was a tyranny of togetherness at table. Damn him, she thought of the man watching her and out of sheer wickedness she looked back at him and smiled. It confounded him as she thought it might, for they had never seen one another before. They would likely never meet again.

She saw that with her response she had arrested his ability to attend to his companion, had made him think only of her, of Charlotte the stranger. He was not handsome. Pallor testified that he wasn't getting enough of all that sun out there even though he was squinting. He had not yet accepted his receding hair line. The woman he was with, from what Charlotte could see of her, could do better. And to think that he sat there assaying Charlotte and her lonely lot. Charlotte had a mind to go over and give him a piece of her mind.

Eating by oneself, without the shield of a book or magazine or newspaper, forces you to think. Solitude is contemplative. Charlotte now supposed that lone wolves like herself came to have richer inner lives than the paired, the shackled. They all thought they knew her but, of course, they couldn't. She knew what she would do. She signed for her bill and then stood and walked toward them.

The man's companion must have read the apprehension in her partner's eye for she turned in her chair to watch Charlotte approach. On seeing her face, Charlotte lit herself up, quickened her pace to their table. The woman, Charlotte saw, was very beautiful.

"I thought it was you guys!" bluffed Charlotte.

"I wasn't…" said the man.

"I wasn't either," Charlotte addressed the woman. "At first I didn't recognize you. Have you done something to your hair?" she said, reasoning that women always had.

"So black, hey?" she said very quickly, "I thought, at first, it made me look…I don't know, Japanese or something." She touched the new do as though it were as delicate as a soap bubble.

"I think it's great, just great. It suits you," Charlotte said, though perhaps it did not.

"Thanks."

Charlotte read once that eyewitness testimony was utterly unreliable, so biased by existing prejudice as to be worse than a chance guess. Charlotte supposed this was to do with the way the human animal's mind would have evolved. There was no benefit in recalling, in photographic detail, the past. People needed to take in only what would help them deal with the future. So they remembered patterns, not what things were, but the *way things were.* That is how they became so judgmental. That is why they calculated, as the flummoxed couple did now, that if someone knew you, then you must know them.

"So, how have you two been?" Charlotte asked, determined to push her stunt, her memory mischief as far as it would go.

The woman at the table looked to her partner. She wanted to find in his expression some hint as to who the hell Charlotte was, where they might have met her, *what her NAME might be*—was she some distant cousin of his, or some chick from the old office? —but she was getting only a reflection of her own ignorance.

"Well. We've been well," she said.

"Oh, that's good," said Charlotte with relief. There was, of course, always something in lives that was "not well" and asking after their welfare drew this out.

"Back together, obviously," the seated woman said, waving a hand back and forth between her partner and herself—him and me, him and me.

"Oh, I didn't know..." Charlotte dared to lay her hand on the unknown woman's shoulder.

"No?" said the man.

"No," said Charlotte. "And...? Oh, I've forgotten his name," this was taunting them, "Last time, remember, you were..."

"Ralph?" he asked.

"Yes. Right. Ralph," said Charlotte, not knowing a thing about any "Ralph".

"Moving around on three legs as good as four now."

"Wow."

"Yeah, were we all as resilient as Ralph."

The man was certain now that his partner remembered who Charlotte was, that she knew the history they shared and would plant a clue for him in her chatter.

"Barry was beside himself with worry," the woman said, "I doubt he'd care that much if it had been me caught up in that snow blower."

"Deb!" the man exclaimed.

So they were Barry and Debbie. They were back together and the cat or dog was ambulatory. They still had most of their coconut cream pie in front of them but they dared not fork any into their mouths because they did not know how casual was their relationship with Charlotte. How could they?

"This is really such an amazing coincidence...if I hadn't got up before dawn to beat the holiday traffic," Charlotte said and looked her watch. "I have to run. Nice to see you, Barry. Really nice. You too, Deb." Charlotte left the onus on them.

"Yes, nice," the man said.

Charlotte finally caught her breath, but was still tremulous, at the highway junction. The couple she had left back at the restaurant would, by now, be arguing over which of them *knew* her. Charlotte took the south ramp, compelled not to go back to Hettie and Dave's cottage but to continue on down the coast toward Bridgewater and Liverpool. Maybe all the way to Yarmouth, for supper and at another table, another couple. Perhaps it would be dark when she finally made it to Chester and they would have gone ahead and eaten without her, worried about her, wondering what Charlotte could have gotten up to, and not having any idea realize, but never say, that they didn't know her at all.

Originally published as a serial in *The Globe and Mail*, August 12-17, 2006.

GLOBAL CONFERENCE

TOWARD SUSTAINABLE DIVERSITY
BETWEEN DIGITAL WORLDS

We wish to acknowledge the ancestral, traditional and unceded Aboriginal territory on which T.S.D.B.D.W. will be held and apologize on behalf of those Aboriginal people for their earlier colonization of the North and South American continents and the subsequent extinction of the mastodon, woolly mammoth and giant sloth through overhunting. We apologize for the Y chromosome and European Culture. The conference is carbon neutral so those attending are asked to keep a detailed dietary log.

**Monday 9AM: Frontiers in
European Designer Eyewear**

This session deals more broadly with the full conference attendee and panelist kit, from techniques for disentangling lanyards and necklaces to using your E.A. or intern as a luggage Sherpa. You are your brand the moment you walk into the conference hotel lobby. Should your dress or shoes always be an on-brand statement colour or has Chrystia Freeland jumped the shark? The unshaven, open shirt with bespoke suit look has been a boon for conference-going men in recent years, should women consider this option? The difficult question of hats. Can adventuresome socks sell your two-piece business suit look as being European while still broadcasting you harbour a deep and genuine remorse over Europe's colonial history? The Lagarde Question: How tanned is too tanned? What to do with your hands when you are on a panel. How to hold a microphone to convey authority without sending an unintended message or TED Talk-style hands-free presentation.

Tuesday 2PM: Tweet That

To remain competitive in the conference world, your message needs constant reinforcement. Exploration of how we can reframe old tautologies with buzz words like "innovation," "engagement," "stakeholder" or simply prefacing keywords with "Bio-" "Inter-" or "Cis-." Compound neologisms like "stakeovation-ment." How is it that the term "digital" retains its vitality yet "cyber" feels old? How to keep a straight face when using terms like "discoverability." Use of various pictographs like emojis to convey a sense of meaning in an increasingly post-literate world.

Wednesday 10AM: Academy Resourcing

Securing and maintaining that highly-compensated university position with little or no teaching respon-sibility is essential to continuing in the global confer-encing network. You need an office with paid staff and a top salary position with benefits at a university (or well-endowed NGO) to sustain your conferenc-ing practice. Consultation contracts with increasingly impoverished Governments are profitable only when your operating costs are subsidized by the profits real-ized from the retail undergraduate education market.

Thursday 10AM: Where to Eat

Every conference-goer has had the crushing experi-ence of returning to the restaurant that was "in" the last time you were in the city only to find it has been discovered by civilians. If Chowhound knows about a place, it is too late. Having a reservation for six to eight at the best new place in town is some of the highest denomination conference currency and puts you out ahead of that most humiliating of conference questions, "Where's everybody going?"

Thursday 2PM: Ins and Outs

In	*Out*
The North	Africa
DXFRYO	LBGTQ
Identity	Socioeconomics
Community Radio	World Cinema
Artisan Barbers	Locovores

Thursday 11PM: Networking and Bonding Bacchanal and Swag Orgy

The traditional conference piss-up and fuckfest not only makes lasting connections, it assures that what happens at the conference stays at the conference by virtue of mutually-assured destruction.

Originally published as "Toward Sustainable Diversity Between Digital Worlds" in *The Overcast*, November 2, 2016.

UNIVERSAL NOTES ON THE FILM'S ROUGH CUT

- This musical score is temporary, right?

- Are we sure we can't afford the rights to that hit song from the film's period? The scene was written with the hit song in mind and it would work really well here.

- X tells Y he/she is going to do that thing and then we immediately see him/her do it. Shouldn't we instead cut straight to X doing it?

- There was such terrific chemistry between X and Y on set, why am not seeing it? Are there better takes?

- I'm sure there are better takes of the stunt.

- Is he kind of old for her?

- The improvised bit here is entertaining but it has nothing to do with the movie so should be cut.

- This line was funnier on the page.

- X takes a dramatic pause in his search the moment before she/he finds what she/he was looking for, which suggests she/he knew where it was all along.

- The kid is terrible/is better than any of the seasoned actors.

- There's going to be CGI there, right? It won't look like that in the release?

- What's up with the sunglasses? It's like I'm watching an episode of "Kabuki Vice." Why are the characters continually taking them off and putting them back on? Or sliding them down their nose to look over them? I wish directors wouldn't let actors have sunglasses.

- Can we lose the scene where X is looking at him/herself in the mirror being "self – reflective"? It's mugging, no?

- That isn't dialogue; it's duelling speeches. Trim them.

- The thing which took so much time and money to make still looks fake and I realize now that we don't need it anyway.

- With what sort of accent is X speaking? It seems to drift from the German-Polish border to the Balkans. And isn't Y supposed to be Danish, would he/she say "Guv'nor!" or "Cor Blimey!" like that? Were those lines in the script? I wish directors wouldn't let actors do accents.

- I wonder about certain period details. I don't believe they had those things back then and even if they did it feels like they shouldn't have.

- By this point in the story they are either fucking or aren't ever going to so people are going to stop caring.

- Cut the improvised stuff here.

- Should we call it a "dramedy"?

- Why did we agree to that wig? I wish directors wouldn't let actors pick their wigs.

- There's a Canada Post super mailbox visible in b.g.

- How did drone photography become so boring so quickly?

- Is it long? It feels long.

- It has three endings. I think it's over when X dies and Y rides/drives/flies/teleports away.

- So many of these problems would have been evident in a table read. Remind me why didn't we have a table read of earlier drafts of the screenplay?

- Can we somehow raise the dramatic stakes?

- I've grown to hate the title—hasn't anyone come up with something better?

- Maybe we go back to the idea of telling the story in a linear, chronological fashion.

- I like the title sequence and the second unit stuff but I have problems with the rest.

Originally published in *The Overcast*, October 15, 2017.

CINEDEMENTIA

El Dorado Journal of Medicine – April 1, 1987

SPECIAL ARTICLE

The Development Of Psychosis After Chronic
Motion Picture Montage – Film Editing And
Madness – Cinedementia A, B, C6

*E. Dermot Lloyd, M.D., Heinrich Richler, M.D.,
Cameron Porter, M.D., Waldo Pidgeon, M.D.,
Louis Jemeal, M.D., Igor Norminski, M.D.,
Paulo Damiro, M .D., Turner Thompson, M.D.*

ABSTRACT. Observations by a number of psychiatrists suggest that the process of film montage or editing contributes to the development of psychosis in practitioners. The disorder is degenerative. Preliminary study results indicate that the severity of the disorder increases with the duration and nature of exposure to montage. Recovery is as yet recorded only in those groups where the disorder has been detected in the early stages of development. In groups where the development of the disorder has gone unchecked and film editing has continued, there has been no response to treatment. Observations of control groups and examinations of case histories suggest that factors related to narrative structure (or its absence) may bear full responsibility for the development of the disorder. Groups with limited exposure to montage have responded well to the Richler-Porter narrative therapy. A panel concludes that the Richler-Porter therapy is the most viable treatment alternative, offering the most hopeful prognosis. The panel calls for the close monitoring of those in the higher risk groups.

An unusually high rate of psychosis has always been noted in the population of Newfoundland, Canada. It has been generally accepted that the prevalence of psychotic disorders on the fog-bound island was the result of readily identifiable environmental factors (poor diet, limited exposure to sunlight, isolation, chronic alcoholism) and hereditary factors (see *El Dorado Journal of Medicine*, June 12, 1979: "Family Swin at the Gene Pool").

This view first came into question in 1982 when Dr. Heinrich Richler noted that societies with a strong oral tradition had an uncommonly high rate of psychotic disorder. Richler travelled to Newfoundland and undertook an exhaustive study of the population in an attempt to establish causality. Richler relied heavily on accounts of psychotic behavior by the local population. These accounts were recorded and published under the title "Lots Of Foolish Ones 'Round Here". An excerpt follows:

> Dr. Richler: You suggested that Heber's behavior was unusual.
>
> Mrs. Fudge: They was all foolish.
>
> Dr. Richler: The entire Noseworthy family?
>
> Mrs. Fudge: Yes, the lot of 'em. I suspects they got it from their father. We called he Foolish Ned. Their mother now, she was right sensible like, never carrying on. But Ned was always tellin' the biggest kind of

lies, 'specially to youngsters or any stunned
enough to believe he.

Dr. Richler: He was a compulsive liar?

Mrs. Fudge: Not lies like you're sayin' now, but
stories, and they only for badness.

Only for badness or because of madness? Dr. Richler
felt that the compulsive construction and relation
of fictional narratives might in some way be linked
to dementia. Richler related these thoughts to Dr.
Cameron Porter in St. John's who, at the time, had
several patients in his care who shared an experience in the film medium. Dr. Porter suggested that
Richler observe filmmakers in the editing process,
where narrative structure was frequently manipu-
lated, in the hope of identifying the development of
symptoms. Richler's subsequent observations were
the first step on the road to a clear understanding
of the disorder. He noted:

*Subject D.N. would quickly become agitated if
he perceived even a minor flaw in the continu-
ity of time and/or space in a motion picture
sequence. The unedited film offered no promise
of resolution, for the material he required was*

not in evidence. Futilely he would attempt to correct the perceived flaw by manipulating the order of the dialogue, inserting non-relevant photographic material (he called these "cut-aways"), planning to insert new dialogue where there was no record of that dialogue, and so on. The process disturbed his perception of chronology and he freely exchanged the terms "before" and "after." As his frustration increased, there was a clear change in his behavior. He began issuing obscenities and made violent references to the material such as "I'll cut the head right off that!" and "I'll kill that in the mix." Convinced that he could find no resolution, he abruptly suggested that we should become intoxicated, whereupon the solution to the narrative problem would come to us as in a dream or visionary experience.

Richler saw immediate evidence that prolonged episodes of motion picture montage resulted in more discontinuous narratives in the films themselves. It appeared that the duration and nature of exposure to montage had a direct link to the seriousness of the disorder.

In one extreme case the subject had been editing the same film for almost ten years. His mental condition was widely reported to have deteriorated considerably over this period. The film narrative that finally emerged from this process was disjointed and absurd. The narrative had no proper chronology, with events from the past, present and probable future being fused into a singular timeframe that clearly existed only in the filmmaker's greatly troubled mind. When I brought this to his attention, he rambled incoherently about "levels of reality" and his own search for meaning. He said, "I have to prove that I exist." The filmmaker saw his ten year effort as a personal odyssey with himself as mythical hero. In as sad a case as I have ever studied, the filmmaker had plainly mistaken chaos for order, order for chaos. He had abandoned reality and truly gone completely insane.

CONTROL GROUP RESULTS. After reviewing a number of such cases and working closely with Dr. Porter and his wards, Richler more firmly established the cause of the disorder (by this time termed Cinedementia or Kinodementia) through closely monitored exposure in control groups.

Group A were asked to edit a short sequence in which an enraged man kills his wife's pet ermine. They were given two working days to assemble the sequence. Richler recorded subtle changes in behavior and moderate anxiety in this group. Three days after the experience, the group's behavior returned to normal.

Group B were asked to edit a longer sequence in which an enraged man, recalling his expulsion from Romania kills his wife's pet ermine and is later tormented by visions of the dead creature.[1] They were given five working days to assemble this sequence. Richler recorded considerable changes in behaviour and extreme anxiety in this group. Violence was reported from one subject. The marked change in behaviour was attributed to the increased complexity of the narrative. The anxiety was the product of the difficult decision making process. Subjects had to decide whether to present the information in chronological order, with Romania first, then the murder of the ermine and finally the vision; or

---

1 The vision was photographically realized by employing miniature sets which created the illusion of a gigantic, threatening ermine. The original, unedited motion pictures for the experiment were produced and directed by Dr. Cameron Porter.

to "flash-back" to the Romanian past as the man killed the ermine (again followed by the vision); or to begin with the vision and then seek out its roots by returning to the ermine's death and Romania. One subject became so distressed that she had to be removed from the experiment after two days. Her roughly edited sequence suggested that the enraged man murdered the ermine and was expelled from Romania for having done so by the victim's gigantic parent (as presented in the dream sequence).

Group C were asked to edit a still longer sequence in which an enraged man, recalling his expulsion from Romania, kills his wife with her own pet ermine during the stage performance of the scenario edited by Group B. A medical ethics committee halted this experiment fearing irreparable consequences for the subjects.

THERAPEUTIC REGIMES. Convinced the cause of Cinedementia had been identified, Richler, in concert with Dr. Porter, set about developing a therapeutic regime for those suffering from the disorder. The treatment demands that the patients first limit daily activity to a bare minimum and at regular intervals relate their activities to a second party. Should they report events or emotions out of chronological order or with embellishment, they are subjected to painful electric shocks from electrodes attached to their fingers and eyelids. Gradually the environment of the patient is enriched and the demands for objective recall increased. In the final stages of the treatment, patients are deliberately exposed to unlikely occurrences such as bleeding electrical outlets, exploding food, talking furniture and so on. If the patient relates these events without trying to establish a rationale or causality, the treatment is judged to have been successful and the patient is released from care. If three months after the termination of treatment the patients imagination appears hopelessly stifled, one can say, in all fairness, that he or she has been cured.

HUMPTY

I must take this opportunity to clarify and apologize for an earlier article, "Just Another Egg Off The Wall," my—perhaps misguided—attempt to inject some levity into what everyone is now calling "L'Affaire Humpty."

It is not true that I implied that Mr. Dumpty was tempting fate by going up to sit on a high wall. Nor was I suggesting that eggs should have restrictions placed on their movements or should not, because of the fragility of their shells, have the same freedoms afforded potatoes, certain squash or any of the foodstuffs from our diverse larder. But I am informed that many of those readers who could not finish the piece for fear of being triggered took that meaning away anyway. I accept responsibility for any pre-triggering the early passages of the item may have induced.

The essence of many of the complaints *The Overcast* received is that I was suggesting that Humpty Dumpty, like a drunk going home across a frozen pond on his quad, had it coming, and that this caused a lot of hurt for eggs everywhere. For the record, let me state categorically that I think all eggs should be free to sit on all walls.

I did not mean to imply that all the King's Horses' and all the King's Persons' efforts to put Humpty Dumpty back together were half-hearted or that they subscribed to some unwritten "you can't make an omelet without breaking a few eggs" policy. I know of nothing to suggest that all the King's Horses and all the King's Persons did less than everything in their power to put Humpty Dumpty back together again. Nor did I ever suggest that Humpty Dumpty, being a white-shelled egg of privilege, got special treatment. The point I was trying to make was that the response time of all the King's Horses and all the King's Persons was inadequate and that given the coming cutbacks, we had all better develop a taste for scrambled. I'm sorry if that didn't come across.

Every drawing I have seen of the tragic event shows Mr. Dumpty in trousers so I believe it is unfair to single me out for anthropomorphizing him. He evidently put on the pants.

My saying the episode left Humpty Dumpty with "face on his egg" was terribly insensitive. I apologize for the comment without reservation.

I quarrel with the assertion that I appropriated the ovate voice. I was once, and some part of me will always be, an egg. Goo goog'joob. Accusations of my egg-washing are half-baked.

Of course it is 2017 and we are cautioned against "provocation" and encouraged to the more wholesome and uplifting "good discussion." Morality squads reviewing work to see that this dictum is honoured should come as no surprise. *The Overcast*'s editors assure me there are so many more people taking pleasure in being outraged than there are items in the paper about which to be outraged that I should apologize and soldier on.

I'm deeply sorry about what happened to Humpty Dumpty. Sure he might have taken unnecessary risks, had a sense of entitlement, tried passing as human, but he was a good egg.

Originally published as "Walking on Eggshells" in *The Overcast*, May 4, 2017.

MODERATES

The declining fortune of Canadian scribblers was lately the subject of a couple of much-talked-about feature pieces in the Toronto papers. It was suggested we abandon dreams of Government support and moonlight like any self-respecting author from Utah. If Canadians don't want to read, who should bother writing for them? Watch the hockey, goes the thinking.

Heeding this advice I submitted the lowest bid on a tender few had seen owing to the closure of the newspapers of record and secured work with CSIS. Their Middle Eastern desk was overextended (some chairs were in the Far East and a filing cabinet was over in

Eastern Europe) and they needed someone to travel to Syria to make contact with "moderate rebels."

I scored a ticket east via Saskatoon on points (the surcharges of $13,892 all but eliminated my profit margin but, unlike a contractor on a megaproject, I resolved to honour my original bid) and thirty-eight hours later found myself in a sook near the Syria-Iraq border. I was looking for a souk but must have bungled my Rosetta Stone Aramaic. After a nap I got over the sook and ventured forth.

I was not so much "abducted" as "given a lift" to the moderate rebels' camp. They are vacillators of The Tepidi Tribe (really more of a service club), many of whom are descendants of French and English Crusaders and so spoke a lugubrious Franglish patois with closed captioning, much like that misunderstood in the Low Ottawa. It wasn't such a bad little rebel camp. There was ample parking, iffy wifi and a coin-operated laundry.

I was subjected to stale sandwiches and Tim Hortons coffee until I confessed I was working for Canadian Intelligence. This admission caused such mirth that I was released from the confines of my musty couch and invited to speak with the rebels' interim (pending a free and fair election) leader.

The moderate rebels are Duvet Muslims, a tolerant branch of the faith said to be the "United Church of Islam," While the women still don the burka for beekeeping, their leader wore only a scrunchy for modesty. She well understood Canada's desire to be near the action of the region's post-colonial clusterfuck, but not so close as to risk getting splattered. The moderate rebels could assist Canada's efforts by making late-morning raids after sleeping in on the weekends, deploying their few locally hand-crafted unguided short-range weapons of limited destruction, and taking and accommodating, as best they could, a few prisoners.

The Military leadership, a committee with a rotating chairpersonship, had all, curiously, trained with the St. John's Sea Cadets, only quitting when they insisted on growing their hair past the collar.

After careful consideration they signed-on, if not to disrupt and destabilize isis or isil or the Ba'athists or Sunni Tribes or Saudi-sponsored Salafists or whoever the hell they are, at least to annoy them with needless paperwork.

Expectations are modest as our new allies are in size as they are in position, moderate, and number in the tens.

LISTEN. I fUlly EXPECTED GROUSING, BUT...

Against the advice of friends and colleagues simply to keep my own counsel and let it go, I am compelled, as one of the much maligned jurors of the Canadian Javelin Prize for Literature, to defend our decision to grant this year's award to Beatrice Miller's *Shield and Surrender*.

Second-guessing juries for literary prizes has lately become something of a sport, so I fully expected grousing over this year's outcome. I did not expect the tone to be so mean-spirited. I've been called a "pseud" and "pompous fake" before. I've been accused of holding petty grudges and being vindictive. You get that in the Academy, and you learn to live with it. But, "the very arsehole of Canlit"? And (in a rather shabby and unimaginative couplet), "an incompetent and compromised fucking wit"? It was sizism to assert that all my taste is in my mouth.

The critical, public and familial response to my own novel, published over a decade ago, had no bearing on this jury process. I'd almost forgotten my book myself. There was no "settling of scores." And, Mr. "Sour Grapes" Johanson, what precisely is an "illitiot"? The term is not in my Oxford English Dictionary (a tool Johanson might have employed to greater effect if he truly aspired to being shortlisted).

My judgment, my very capacity for reason, have been called into question. I am being ridiculed for merely having a point of view. I now see why the first 16 or so (I've heard and discount estimates as high as 80) persons approached to jury the prize refused the honour.

The assertion that only people with nothing better to do can dedicate the time required to read several hundred novels is untrue. That one's schedule should have the occasional lacuna is natural, that it should have occurred when the prize was to be decided was kismet. It happened that I was on sabbatical and was obliged, because of an injury, to keep my foot elevated. Fellow juror Jack Smyth was, in fact, terrifically busy yet leapt at the opportunity to contribute. For the record: I went through every submission, cover to cover, even if I knew that I would never, under any circumstance, vote for that particular title before I'd read a word of it. I am nothing if not fair. I cannot vouch for the diligence of the other jurors, one of whom is getting on in years and so having trouble with his sight.

Of course, in the end, it is an entirely subjective affair. No single book can be said, in any sort of absolute terms, to be that year's "best." But on balance, given the variable criteria and fuzzy assumptions the jury was working with, *Shield and Surrender* is as deserving (or the least undeserving) as any title.

One can always say that others could, even should, have won. Titles that might have been on the shortlist were not, but that is a peril of the procedure. Is un-inclusion akin to exclusion? I don't think so. Only five finalists can be announced so the presence of one or two titles that probably should not be there can, I suppose, be said, by virtue of some mathematical conjuring I do not quite fathom, to keep 20 or 30 more deserving titles from consideration, but this is not the point I wish to address. (I will admit that Marvin Bourne's *Borealis* probably should not have been there, but Mr. Bourne was, at the time the shortlist was being drawn up, severely infected and possessed of a life's body of work that had not yet been sufficiently recognized. That the infection finally cleared up in no way affected the jury's ultimate decision not to award him the Javelin.)

The oft-observed absence of Philip Russet's withering satire *Trail of Crumbs* from this year's shortlist is perhaps an appropriate counter to Bourne's presence, while at the same time redressing Russet's undeserved 1992 shortlisting for his comparatively weaker, though handsomely packaged first novel, *Were You Red?* Furthermore, satire, by its very nature, induces discomfort and doubt in the reader. How successful can such a lampoon be if it has garnered the approbation of five jurors? Surely Russet must see this rebuff as artistic success. Likewise his dreadful sales. In any event, nobody in Canadian letters can bear Russet, he's so smug.

Everyone can acknowledge that Geraldine Penning's *Lip Felt* is an exceptional piece and of a standard for the shortlist. Unfortunately, it was late in the day when it was discussed and Lynn Parmenter's *Crayola*, a similar sort of book, had already made our tentative list in the morning. Besides, Penning is very young, with many years ahead of her to win awards. (Think of poor Bourne, easily at his threescore and 10, infected, without even a regional award yet to his name!) If Penning does not subsequently publish anything of merit, then we can be said to have been sage in not naming her. If she does, then a future jury can deal with her.

That there has been, every year of the prize, one title from a small press on the shortlist is entirely coincidental and not tokenism. To suggest otherwise is as absurd as supposing (despite what I concede looks to be overwhelming evidence) that there are unspoken regional, ethnic and genre quotas. In fact, quite the opposite is the case; I will allow readers a glimpse inside the jury room and reveal that a very meritorious work of historical fiction was kept from this year's list because there was a feeling that there were too many such books on last year's list, as well as the lists of all the years before that. And, has anyone ever considered that the dimensions of the "small" presses owe something to their output?

Alan Steves's and Diane Foster's good looks were immaterial to their being shortlisted. It is a commercial reality, however superficial, that the author photo is one of the first introductions of book to reader. If a masturbatory fantasy brings more people to literature, what harm is done? In the end, the reader is left with the book in hand. If appearances counted for anything in the awarding of the prize, how is it that Melvin Hewer has thrice been shortlisted? My characterization of Ms. Foster as "delectable as a chocolate" can, and must, be divorced from my appreciation of her growing talents as an authoress.

Harvey Renfield's *A List of Attributes* was not excluded because he had sexual relations with the wife, sister and, most unforgivably, the literary agent, of my fellow juror Jack Smyth. Jack was a paragon of objectivity and convinced us to exclude *Attributes* on the basis of his thorough cataloguing of that book's failings.

To address some other "really should have been shortlisteds":

- *The Complete Soviet Acronyms*, Peter Keating — far too difficult
- *Pussy Fart*, Alma Dink — far too pornographic
- *Blah, Blah, Blah, Fucking Blah*, Irving Candow — far too angry
- *The Full Lake of Woe*, Alice Duncan — far too depressing
- *Herb's Ass*, Arvo Kanelmaki — far too gay
- *Tune Thy Rills*, Hubert Williams — far too East Coast (far too gay?)

The most commonly voiced knock against *Shield and Surrender* is that the prose is rather "conventional," "controlled" to the point of being "stolid," and that Beatrice Miller has written what is essentially the same book many times before. This I will not argue. In fact, I believe such to be one of the novel's greatest strengths.

The language reflects the Southern Ontario setting, as does the reticence of its characters and the near-absolute humourlessness of the story. The people that work the land around the lakes have never been known for garrulousness or lightheartedness. They are laconic people of Scots and English extraction. They are reluctant to complain or to bray. Are those quarrelling with the jury's decision saying they would prefer prose that is "out of control?" It is time that boredom and its experience, particularly in the context of the Canadian novel, is recognized as an aesthetic.

I dispute the claim the winning book is prudish. There is congress, albeit in the past, and under heavy blankets in a room far away, in a remote cottage on Georgian Bay. This is, to my mind, more evidence of the author's craft. This is writing about sex for those uncomfortable with, and in, the act. When Verna, the protagonist, sits for her portrait those long winter months, who could not see her reveries about a youth in the orchards as erotic, even if it is eros of the more arid sort.

The most noxious criticism levelled at *Shield and Surrender*, particularly in this day and age, is that it is, like all Beatrice Miller's oeuvre, "women's fiction." The fact has to be faced that a great majority of the readers of fiction now are women and that to write about male experience or for a male audience is to write without witness. (What has become of the masculine readership is another discussion, though I speculate that they are either off doing something in the garage or having a nap.) That *Shield and Surrender* is about the unhappy lives of girls in Ontario speaks to its timeliness, it's connecting to the estrogenic zeitgeist of these times.

I will not dignify with a response suggestions that there was some sort of unspoken quid pro quo going on, and that my collected essays *The Great Evacuation* is being published by McGaggle-Roherty as a reward for selecting a title published by that house.

Finally, I do not think I am violating the confidence of my fellow jurors in revealing that *Shield and Surrender* was the first choice of no one, but a satisfactory compromise candidate for all. The non-winners (an admittedly clumsy term) can take comfort in the knowledge that they each, but for one, had a champion, as well as an ardent, unmoving opponent dismissing their work as utter shit, throwing temper tantrums, threatening to derail the whole process in a sordid public display of dissension if they didn't have their way. I will never again accept such an assignment and I think I have read my last work of fiction for a very long time. I was beginning to find the form, with its grown-up games of make-believe, frivolous anyway. If, as widely reported, the novel is dead, maybe it's time someone buried it before it stinks the place up. Truth be told, I prefer a good history.

Originally published in *The Globe and Mail*, November 5, 2005.

MARITIME
MONOTONY
WHERE THE EXCITEMENT
NEVER STARTS

Cranstock, New Brunswick, is not, as is often claimed, the most boring town in Canada's Maritime provinces. While its Festival of Sand is among the least exciting events in the Atlantic region, the town falls somewhere in the middle of the range of lacklustre area destinations. Cranstock cannot even assert that it is the most boring town in New Brunswick, a title held for many, many, many years (too many to bother counting) by Addleby, the historical museum of which displays a copy of the 1968 phone book, the last year a separate edition was issued for the county. Frestover, Nova Scotia, situated at the mouth of the turbid, sluggish, and meandering Western River, on the featureless Northern Shore, was long considered one of the most uninteresting places in all of Canada, let alone the Atlantic provinces, until, in 2001, a fair-sized sinkhole appeared near the municipal boundary and a hobby farmer nearby acquired a llama.

While not technically part of the Maritimes, three towns in Newfoundland should be mentioned. There is Belant, where a train was once to stop until a proposed aggregate quarry fell through, and Squashberry Cove, no longer included on maps (despite a recent increase in population to 112 people or 98 souls). Wilty Bay, Newfoundland, is, by uninteresting coincidence, the birthplace of two provincial cabinet ministers who both held the portfolio of Culture, Recreation and Youth; and while each served with such little distinction as to deserve notice here, they were occasionally in the company of some fast-talking shysters. That Shelton preserves the architecturally nondescript and unfurnished Youver House as birthplace of little-known regional poet Leo McMackie recommends it as a candidate for Prince Edward Island's most tedious place, but this has to be considered in light of Poseydale's numbing almost-flatness and the closure of the local store. The archaeological dig at Lower Point, Nova Scotia revealed no earlier settlement by European or indigenous peoples. Recently discovered documents suggest there is no longer any reason to believe that the wife of former Prime Minister John Diefenbaker, Olive, actually visited Loamingville Extension. Knollview is almost equidistant from Turnington and the intersection of the Trans-Canada Highway and Route 16. Owing to the construction of the Borden Bypass, there has been a 96 percent reduction in traffic through the Hanover Junction.

Middleville, Nova Scotia, is just that—no more, no less—which might be noteworthy if the same could not be said for a town of the same name and identical circumstance in New Brunswick. These two towns, separated by hundreds of kilometres, are also similar in many other inconsequential respects, a fact of some note—thereby disqualifying it—to persons with an interest in matters trivial. It is not even ironic that two places cannot both be "the middle of nowhere."

Pointe Rien's remoteness is enough to merit a geographic footnote even if the gravel road to its uninterrupted, narcotic vistas of the placid and perpetually fogbound Baie d'Ennui make it éviter le détour. The Department of Fisheries and Oceans has withdrawn the designation "bore" from the tidal action in the shallow bay.

Low-level excitement, in the form of petty crime committed by teens and the adulterous shenanigans of their parents, disqualifies the outwardly dull bedroom communities Mount Villard, Falmouth, and Lower Georgeville. Mount Villard is really little more than a hill…well, "hillock"—okay, "mound."

The influx of summering Toronto literati and CBC types makes for some pretty monotonous times in sleepy Mud Bay, but this is merely seasonal tedium.

Longbridge, New Brunswick's "Instructional Videotape Triannual" has evolved into a fascinating event.

Everyone, and I mean everyone, will be familiar with the handcrafted whirligigs of Dalton, New Brunswick, but it must be remembered that there are those with an interest, however passing, in folk art.

Though "Buoy Week" does not liven up things in Dillpool, Nova Scotia, there are "an awful lot of flies" on account of the meal plant, which is, at least, something. The village has also twice been awarded a certificate of merit by the Canadian Dental Association for the council's successful efforts to promote flossing.

While the goods on offer at the flea market held every other Tuesday in nearby Outerton are almost never in demand, something potentially curious sometimes, if rarely, shows up. Such was the case only two years ago when a carton of vintage, canister-type vacuum-cleaner bags turned out to have been unopened, causing if not a stir, then a quiver.

Notwithstanding declining attendance, given the success of the nap-a-thon, they have rebuilt the United Church at Harwell in very much the same style as its predecessor.

Kerrington, Prince Edward Island, surely gets honourable mention for its potato sandwiches, but this is a foodstuff nowhere as flavourless as the dough-filled pies of Maramatouche, New Brunswick.

Owing to its orderly and perfectly regular numbered street system, they say it's impossible to lose one's way in tiny Calondee, New Brunswick, all the inhabitants of which are still direct descendants of the original Scots Presbyterian founders.

While the author appreciates the thoroughness with which officials responded to his queries, details concerning the hamlet of Bobbington are still too vague to be accurately assessed.

The queue of contenders to be foremost of the least is long and can fairly be said to be "not moving at all," for the dullest town in the Maritimes remains Wentbury, the only notable feature (and not a distinguishing one) of which is that it was founded in 1789. The citizenry of Wentbury remain unable to imagine what sort of excitement might liven things up. The municipal plan, adopted in 2002, remains on track. The infrastructure is holding up somewhat better than anticipated, and the town council has announced a modest surplus. Wentbury was spared the flooding experienced to the east and was not nearly as hot and dry last summer as towns were to the west. For the sixth straight year the Wentbury Riders placed fourth in their division, which was not too bad. The anticipated exchange student from the Czech Republic had to cancel on account of having contracted the mumps. The town almost lost the title of most boring when it last year briefly considered adopting the motto "No Complaints," but in the end a respectable, but by no means overwhelming, majority of the people of Wentbury decided against this.

Originally published in *The Walrus*, December 12, 2006.

AFTERWORD
BAG OF HAMMERS

The first comedy I wrote was for *The Muse*, the student newspaper of Memorial University of Newfoundland. I pounded out a few cringe-worthy feature pieces and the occasional poorly informed film or album review on the paper's old manual Underwoods; but my saucy stuff was better. It always got a few laughs and the occasional complaint of hurt feelings, usually from a student council which in those days had a reputation for being the Newfoundland and Labrador Provincial Government in training. We at *The Muse* understood it was our responsibility to give them grief.

In the fall of 1980, *The Muse* was part of a largely unorganized student crusade to do something about The Parkway, a four-lane highway which, owing to a kind of haphazard urban "planning" endemic to St. John's, bisected the campus. Crossing the road was perilous and the student body wanted a remedy.

The Muse didn't want to let the issue die, so running a story about it as often as possible was a priority. But there was only so much one could say: the road was in the wrong place and presented a real danger to students, a safe crossing needed to be provided and soon. That was it. I took up the baton for the week of the October 17th edition reporting on an imagined "Parkway Safari" motor-sport event in which drivers tore around campus trying to strike and kill students with their cars, scoring points as they did so. I enlisted a couple of pals to pose as victims for grisly photos of the contest. The piece did what I still suppose good satire does, issue a warning about where a stupid behavior will land us if we don't smarten up. The paper was distributed throughout the campus in the morning. That afternoon a Memorial University student, a young woman full of promise, Judy Lynn Ford, was struck and killed by a car on The Parkway. I thought the tragedy proved the point of my piece. Some on campus, unaware that it had been written and printed before the accident, judged it, I can't say unfairly if they believed it was in response, in horrendously bad taste.

Bad taste often lends satire vitality. As it can be a knife or a skewer, satire can also be a blunt instrument. It can be a cudgel, a hammer. Thus the title of this collection. We say in Newfoundland "Foolish as a bag of hammers" to mean something or someone ridiculous. In other places there is "ugly as a bag of hammers" to mean that which is lumpen, misshapen, unwieldy. All that can be said of comic and satiric prose.

The outrage over the Parkway piece didn't much bother me, my heart was colder then.

Energies soon found focus in a spontaneous act of civil disobedience, students marching across a crosswalk on The Parkway in an uninterrupted looping line so as to permanently arrest the flow of traffic. The cops arrived and handled things poorly, the protest escalating to the point where they considered it best to beat a retreat. Barricades were erected, the students occupied the highway for a glorious weekend until commitments were given (and promptly honoured) to build an elevated "pedway" over the road.

After three years majoring in Chemistry at Memorial, I abruptly changed course and enrolled in Film School at Concordia University's Fine Arts Faculty. I came then to write comedy for film and television. I wrote a couple of feature-film screenplays including the adaptation of my novel *Rare Birds* and a bunch of episodes of the television industry satire *Made in Canada*. I kept up writing for print media and wrote for the stage.

I spent the most creatively rewarding five years of my life writing, with Steve Palmer and Mack Furlong, the CBC Radio show *The Great Eastern*, a program I have no hesitation declaring among the very best examples of scripted radio in the history of that medium. *The Great Eastern* was a tremendous success, critically lauded, with a large audience but was a more sophisticated sort of comedy than the CBC brass envisaged for a show coming out of Newfoundland. Yucks of a simpler sort were expected from yokels in the colonies. We were told to make the show, "more accessible" and "less foreground." (CBC Radio's higher-ups have always held the listenership in low regard, thinking them incapable of appreciating challenging material.) A CBC Vice-President, the very man who took the considerable risk programming the show, cautioned us "No more jokes about French philosophers." We paid him no heed and CBC canned us one season before the project was completed. I wrote a novel, *Easy To Like* that was, in part, a satire about the CBC and put it thus:

"The green-lit show has a Newfoundland theme, that's all. It's going to be shot in Halifax—they've kissed my ass raw looking for something to keep the plant open. I'll make them produce it in St. John's if you want. I'm the president. I'll shut down the Halifax studio instead—they've got the navy, they can't complain."

"What's the show?"

"*Tiny Newfies.*"

"*Tiny Newfies?*"

"It's fun. We tested the pilot. Canadians love tiny Newfies."

"What about Newfoundlanders?"

"As long as it's about them, they're fine with it. You'll find they're needy that way."

Things got worse at CBC Radio. They no longer produce original scripted material or music. The service is a shadow of its former self, reduced to vapid chatter, testimonials of victimhood, and "spinning discs." It's cheap, intellectually lazy and, inexcusably, boring.

Over the years I've continued to write humourous pieces for print in *The Walrus*, *The Globe and Mail*, *The Newfoundland Quarterly*, and *The Overcast* and they form the bulk of that which is included in this collection.

How have things changed since I started out almost forty years ago?

The theft of content facilitated by an unregulated Internet has made earning a living creating things more precarious. In 2007 I read, I cannot recall where, the ominous prediction that anything which could be mechanically reproduced would no longer have any value in trade. That seems to be coming true. There are fewer printed pages for which to write. More eye-hours are dedicated to phones. There is a real worry that fiction will only be written by those teaching or taking Creative Writing courses, a thought almost too horrible to contemplate.

Some fuzzy thinkers have lately theorized that satire is inherently conservative either because it mocks the "non-normative" or, in having fun making fun, "normalizes" the misdeeds of a ruling elite. But this is confusing spoof—Alex Baldwin's Trump say—with satire. Satire would, instead, have explored how the self-satisfaction of the Obama administration and the entitlement of the Clinton campaign made them blind to the discontent of those to whom the empty promises of "Hope" and "Change" had been given and so paved the way for the election of the Horror Clown.

In four decades what is funny and how comedy works hasn't changed much at all. The audience has; it's grown timid. The pieties of political correctness have scared people off that which is transgressional. People have become afraid to laugh lest it be heard as laughter "at" something. We are surrendering our right and occasional need to be offended. I find the term "Newfie" offensive and, as a writer, deploy it as such. Mores evolve, and what is "acceptable" changes all the time. Someone sometimes needs to say that which is unacceptable. Sometimes the State, the Temple, or the People's Committee on Virtue must be challenged. Most insidiously a climate of censure begets self-censorship. Inquiry is stifled.

So it was that two bright accomplished professional people, on separate occasions, told me they put down my novel *Today I Learned It Was You* because they were "afraid of where it was going." At the center of that novel is a report that a one-time thespian sleeping rough in a public park in St. John's is "transitioning" from man to deer. Spoiler alert: he isn't doing any such thing. The ridiculous proposition that he is, a bit of dark mischief by another character in the novel, is embraced by a gullible and wishful public to such a degree that confessing the deed becomes unthinkable. Those readers "afraid of where it was going" never read far enough to grasp that the central joke was that very fear. And it is not just discomfiting fiction from which people are averting their eyes, it's also from those facts which don't fit their tribe's narrative or mythology. That's where we are now.

"Satire is what closes on Saturday night" said George S. Kaufman, and indeed it's never going to be big box office, it's never awards bait. It's bound, if it's any good at all, to ruffle feathers, but it has a social function to say that which isn't being said and, at its highest level, to think and speak the unthinkable. Satire is a distant early warning system. Without it the most unlikely and absurd consequences befall those who haven't imagined the world at its most preposterous.

The speech police, these days as likely to come from the smoldering ruins of the political left or The Academy as from the Church or the Mosque or the Presidential palace, are making it more difficult and more dangerous to sound the alarm. If there was ever a time to reach into the bag for a hammer it's now.

Happy Valley–Goose Bay,
September 21, 2017

ACKNOW LEDGEMENTS

Thanks to the brave and hardworking editors who have commissioned pieces from me over the years: Elling Lien, Chad Pelley, Sarmishta Subramanian, Doug Saunders, and Joan Sullivan. Thanks to Charlie Tomlinson and Gerry Porter for reading early drafts and setting me straight. And thanks to James Langer for sorting through and selecting the articles that appear on these pages.

Edward Riche is the author of the novels *Rare Birds, The Nine Planets, Easy to Like*, and *Today I learned it was You*. He has scripted for television, three feature films, and six plays. His articles have appeared in *The Globe and Mail*, *Macleans*, and *The Walrus*. He has received five Writers Guild of Canada Awards, the Actra National Radio Award, the Winterset and Thomas Raddell Prizes for literature, and an Atlantic Journalism Award. In 2004, Riche was named the Newfoundland and Labrador Artist of the Year. He lives in St. John's.

www.ingramcontent.com/pod-product-compliance
Lightning Source LLC
Chambersburg PA
CBHW061524020726
47502CB00006B/2216